S E R I E S

A NavPress Bible study on the book of

NAVPRESS ◗™

A MINISTRY OF THE NAVIGATORS
P.O. BOX 35001, COLORADO SPRINGS, COLORADO 80935

The Navigators is an international Christian organization. Our mission is to reach, disciple, and equip people to know Christ and to make Him known through successive generations. We envision multitudes of diverse people in the United States and every other nation who have a passionate love for Christ, live a lifestyle of sharing Christ's love, and multiply spiritual laborers among those without Christ.

NavPress is the publishing ministry of The Navigators. NavPress publications help believers learn biblical truth and apply what they learn to their lives and ministries. Our mission is to stimulate spiritual formation among our readers.

Printed in the United States of America

15 16 17 18 19 20 21 22 23 / 00 99 98 97 96

CONTENTS

ACKNOWLEDGMENTS

The LIFECHANGE series has been produced through the coordinated efforts of a team of Navigator Bible study developers and NavPress editorial staff, along with a nationwide network of fieldtesters.

SERIES EDITOR: KAREN LEE-THORP

HOW TO USE THIS STUDY

Objectives

Most guides in the LIFECHANGE series of Bible studies cover one book of the Bible. Although the LIFECHANGE guides vary with the books they explore, they share some common goals:

1. To provide you with a firm foundation of understanding and a thirst to return to the book;

2. To teach you by example how to study a book of the Bible without structured guides;

3. To give you all the historical background, word definitions, and explanatory notes you need, so that your only other reference is the Bible;

4. To help you grasp the message of the book as a whole;

5. To teach you how to let God's Word transform you into Christ's image.

Each lesson in this study is designed to take 60 to 90 minutes to complete on your own. The guide is based on the assumption that you are completing one lesson per week, but if time is limited you can do half a lesson per week or whatever amount allows you to be thorough.

Flexibility

LIFECHANGE guides are flexible, allowing you to adjust the quantity and depth of your study to meet your individual needs. The guide offers many optional questions in addition to the regular numbered questions. The optional questions, which appear in the margins of the study pages, include the following:

Optional Application. Nearly all application questions are optional; we hope you will do as many as you can without overcommitting yourself.

For Thought and Discussion. Beginning Bible students should be able to handle these, but even advanced students need to think about them. These questions frequently deal with ethical issues and other biblical principles. They often offer cross-references to spark thought, but the references do not give obvious answers. They are good for group discussions.

For Further Study. These include: a) cross-references that shed light on a topic the book discusses, and b) questions that delve deeper into the passage. You can omit them to shorten a lesson without missing a major point of the passage.

If you are meeting in a group, decide together which optional questions to prepare for each lesson, and how much of the lesson you will cover at the next meeting. Normally, the group leader should make this decision, but you might let each member choose his or her own application questions.

As you grow in your walk with God, you will find the LIFECHANGE guide growing with you—a helpful reference on a topic, a continuing challenge for application, a source of questions for many levels of growth.

Overview and Details

The study begins with an overview of John. The key to interpretation is context—what is the whole passage or book *about?*—and the key to context is purpose—what is the author's *aim* for the whole work? In lesson one you will lay the foundation for your study of John by asking yourself, "Why did the author (and God) write the book? What did they want to accomplish? What is the book about?"

In lessons two through twenty-two you will analyze successive passages of John in detail. Thinking about how a paragraph fits into the overall goal of the book will help you to see its purpose. Its purpose will help you see its meaning. Frequently reviewing a chart or outline of the book will enable you to make these connections.

In lesson twenty-two you will review John, returning to the big picture to see whether your view of it has changed after closer study. Review will also strengthen your grasp of major issues and give you an idea of how you have grown from your study.

Kinds of Questions

Bible study on your own—without a structured guide—follows a progression. First you observe: What does the passage *say*? Then you interpret: What does the passage *mean*? Lastly you apply: How does this truth *affect* my life?

Some of the "how" and "why" questions will take some creative thinking, even prayer, to answer. Some are opinion questions without clearcut right answers; these will lend themselves to discussions and side studies.

Don't let your study become an exercise of knowledge alone. Treat the passage as God's Word, and stay in dialogue with Him as you study. Pray, "Lord, what do You want me to see here?" "Father, why is this true?" "Lord, how does this apply to my life?"

It is important that you write down your answers. The act of writing clarifies your thinking and helps you to remember.

Study Aids

A list of reference materials, including a few notes of explanation to help you make good use of them, begins on page 211. This guide is designed to include enough background to let you interpret with just your Bible and the guide. Still, if you want more information on a subject or want to study a book on your own, try the references listed.

Scripture Versions

Unless otherwise indicated, the Bible quotations in this guide are from the New International Version of the Bible. Other versions cited are the Revised Standard Version (RSV), the New American Standard Bible (NASB), and the King James Version (KJV).

Use any translation you like for study, preferably more than one. A paraphrase such as The Living Bible is not accurate enough for study, but it can be helpful for comparison or devotional reading.

Memorizing and Meditating

A psalmist wrote, "I have hidden your word in my heart that I might not sin against you" (Psalm 119:11). If you write down a verse or passage that challenges or encourages you, and reflect on it often for a week or more, you will find it beginning to affect your motives and actions. We forget quickly what we read once; we remember what we ponder.

When you find a significant verse or passage, you might copy it onto a card to keep with you. Set aside five minutes during each day just to think about what the passage might mean in your life. Recite it over to yourself, exploring its meaning. Then, return to your passage as often as you can during your day, for a brief review. You will soon find it coming to mind spontaneously.

For Group Study

A group of four to ten people allows the richest discussions, but you can adapt this guide for other sized groups. It will suit a wide range of group types, such as home Bible studies, growth groups, youth groups, and businessmen's studies. Both new and experienced Bible students, and new and mature Christians, will benefit from the guide. You can omit or leave for later years any questions you find too easy or too hard.

The guide is intended to lead a group through one lesson per week. However, feel free to split lessons if you want to discuss them more thoroughly. Or, omit some questions in a lesson if preparation or discussion time is limited. You can always return to this guide for personal study later. You will be able to discuss only a few questions at length, so choose some for discussion and others for background. Make time at each discussion for members to ask about anything they didn't understand.

Each lesson in the guide ends with a section called "For the group." These sections give advice on how to focus a discussion, how you might apply the lesson in your group, how you might shorten a lesson, and so on. The group leader should read each "For the group" at least a week ahead so that he or she can tell the group how to prepare for the next lesson.

Each member should prepare for a meeting by writing answers for all of the background and discussion questions to be covered. If the group decides not to take an hour per week for private preparation, then expect to take at least two meetings per lesson to work through the questions. Application will be very difficult, however, without private thought and prayer.

Two reasons for studying in a group are accountability and support. When each member commits in front of the rest to seek growth in an area of life, you can pray with one another, listen jointly for God's guidance, help one another to resist temptation, assure each other that the other's growth matters to you, use the group to practice spiritual principles, and so on. Pray about one another's commitments and needs at most meetings. Spend the first few minutes of each meeting sharing any results from applications prompted by previous lessons. Then discuss new applications toward the end of the meeting. Follow such sharing with prayer for these and other needs.

If you write down each other's applications and prayer requests, you are more likely to remember to pray for them during the week, ask about them at the next meeting, and notice answered prayers. You might want to get a notebook for prayer requests and discussion notes.

Notes taken during discussion will help you to remember, follow up on ideas, stay on the subject, and clarify a total view of an issue. But don't let note-taking keep you from participating. Some groups choose one member at each meeting to take notes. Then someone copies the notes and distributes them at the next meeting. Rotating these tasks can help include people. Some groups have someone take notes on a large pad of paper or erasable marker board (preformed shower wallboard works well), so that everyone can see what has been recorded.

Pages 213-214 list some good sources of counsel for leading group studies. The *Small Group Letter,* published by NavPress, is unique, offering insights from experienced leaders every other month.

OVERVIEW

Introducing John's Gospel

Jesus' Ministry

Leon Morris compares "John's Gospel to a pool in which a child may wade and an elephant can swim."[1] On the one hand, it is commonly given to new believers and even inquirers to examine the foundations of Christian faith. It is a favorite for the simple faith of simple folk. On the other hand, "years of close study of this Gospel do not leave one with a feeling of having mastered it, but rather with the conviction that it is still 'strange, restless, and unfamiliar.'"[2] Like Him whom it portrays, this book readily welcomes the humble and endlessly challenges the wise.

First impressions

You should have a chance to form first impressions of a book before someone tells you what you should see. The best way to do this is to read John's Gospel through, in one sitting if possible. Read quickly for an overall view, not stopping to ponder the details. Notice the passage subtitles in your Bible, if it includes them.

Before you begin reading, look over questions 1 through 7. Keep them in mind as you go through the Gospel. You can list repeated words as you read, or underline them in your Bible. You can also jot notes about your first impressions in this study guide, a notebook, or the margin of your Bible.

Study Skill—Overview

It is wise to come to some tentative sense of what a book is about and what its author is trying to accomplish before examining isolated passages in detail. The first question we strive to answer as students of the Bible is, "What message was the author trying to convey to the original readers?" This question helps us focus on the intent of the author so that we will get out of the book what the Holy Spirit intended.

We approach this question by reading the book through one or more times, looking for first impressions, repeated words and ideas, and the author's feelings about his topic and his readers. Then, we sketch a general outline of the book by giving titles to each chapter or major section. Having made these sorts of observations, we can have some preliminary opinions about the author's purpose.

---

1. What are your first impressions of this book? (For example, what is it about? What overall impression does it give you of Jesus? What do you notice about the way the author writes? Is there a lot of action, description, dialogue, doctrinal teaching, instructions for behavior, or what? Is it easy or hard to follow?)

_____

_____

_____

_____

_____

2. What key words and phrases appear over and over?

_____

_____

_____

_____

_____

3. If you are familiar with any of the other three Gospels, how is John's Gospel like and unlike them?

_____

_____

_____

_____

_____

Study Skill—Outline

A broad outline of a book often helps you see at a glance how it is put together and what it is meant to say. You make a broad outline by giving a title to each chapter (sometimes to part of a chapter or to several chapters). Good titles accomplish these things:
1. They help you recall the content of the passage.
2. They are unique to that passage.
To come up with a good title, ask yourself, "What was the author's purpose in including this section? How does this section fit his overall purpose for writing?"

4. Give a title to each of the following sections:

1:1-18 _____

1:19-51 _____

2:1-11 _____

2:12-25 _____

3:1-21 _____

3:22-36 _____

4:1-42 _____

4:43-54 _____

5:1-47 _____

6:1-71 _____

7:1-53 _____

8:1-59 _____

9:1-41 _____

10:1-21 _____

10:22-42 _____

11:1-57 _____

12:1-11 _____

12:12-50 _____

13:1-38 _____

14:1-31 _____

15:1-27 _____

16:1-33 _____

17:1-26 _____

18:1–19:42 _____

20:1-31 _____

21:1-25 _____

5. Another clue to the author's intent, perhaps the most obvious one, is what he says explicitly about it. What do you learn about John's purpose from 20:30-31?

_____

_____

_____

6. Now that you've made some initial observations, try to pull your thoughts together into a summary statement. What would you say was John's main purpose in writing this book?

_____

_____

_____

_____

7. Did this overview suggest questions you would like answered and topics you would like to pursue further as you study the book in detail? If so, jot them down to serve as personal objectives for your study.

_____

_____

_____

_____

_____

Study Skill—Application

James 1:22 and 2 Timothy 3:16-17 remind us of the primary reason we study God's Word—to let it affect our lives so that we will become fully the people God desires. Therefore, the last step of Bible study should always be to ask yourself, "What difference should this passage make to my life? How should it make me want to think or act?" Application will require time, thought, prayer, and perhaps even discussion with another person.

At times you may find it most productive to concentrate on one specific application, giving it careful thought and prayer. At other times you may want to list many implications a passage of Scripture has for your life, meditating on them all for several days before you choose one for concentrated prayer and action. Do whatever helps you to take to heart and act on what the passage says.

---

8. Look over your notes so far, and ask the Lord to help you see one or two areas He wants to focus on in affecting your life. Write down those general areas or specific ways in which you want to change and grow.

_____

_____

_____

_____

_____

_____

9. Is there anything you want to do about this during the coming week? If so, jot down your plans.

_____

_____

_____

_____

_____

A Gospel of John?

Few scholars today, besides conservative evangelicals, believe the ancient tradition that the Apostle John wrote this Gospel. Readers interested in this debate should consult the commentaries.[3] Despite the current fashion of opinion, the evidence points to a Palestinian Jew who had access to much eyewitness testimony about Jesus' life, who had substantial authority in some part of the Church, and who wrote before 100 AD. The unanimous opinion of the Church from 180 AD onward (we have no clear records before then) was that this person was John the Apostle.

When did John write his Gospel? Modern scholars no longer find any good reason to date the book after 100 AD, and some evidence suggests before 70 AD.[4] Anytime toward the end of John's life seems reasonable.

Four Gospels

Gospel is an Old English word that means "good news." It translates the Greek word *euangelion* (*eu-*, "good" and *angelion*, "message"), which also gives us words like "evangelist" and is related to words like "angel." When the first Christians wanted to record the "good news" about the Man who was God, none of the familiar forms of literature seemed suitable. The Christians didn't write the kinds of biographies or sacred texts that were common in Greek or Jewish culture. Instead, they created a new form: the Gospel.

Many collections of Jesus' words and deeds were composed in the century after His death, but God uniquely inspired four men to write the Gospels that would bear His authority. The early Christians took time and trouble to discern authentic from spurious records of Jesus' life. The books of Matthew, Mark, and Luke are called the *Synoptic* (one view) Gospels because they have much more material in common than any of them has with John.

The Synoptics focus on Jesus' ministry in Galilee and His last week in Jerusalem, but John highlights Jesus' ministry in Jerusalem during several visits over the space of three years. John omits Jesus' birth, His human ancestry, His baptism, the Transfiguration, almost all of Jesus' parables, the bread and wine of the Last Supper, and the agony in Gethsemane. Only one of the miracles John records (the feeding of the five thousand) is in all three of the other Gospels. Instead of the short, pithy parables and sayings in the Synoptics, John gives us long discourses on subjects related to Jesus' identity and mission. He records seven "I am" statements by Jesus, none of which are in the Synoptics. Why the differences?

14

Even an ordinary man is usually seen differently by different friends. We have accounts of Socrates by two different disciples that make one wonder if they are describing the same man. The Synoptics seem to be based on the memories of Peter, Matthew, Mary and others, while John's Gospel seems to be his own recollections independent of theirs. God apparently prompted John to show us another face of Jesus.

Many people have remarked on how different Jesus' teaching in John is from His teaching in the Synoptics. Yet there are many possible explanations. For example, the parables and short sayings we find in the Synoptics are the kind of public teaching that rabbis used to make their students memorize. First-century students didn't take notes on paper; people thought you hadn't really learned a thing until you had memorized it. So, the Sermon on the Mount, the parables, etc. are probably material Jesus made His disciples commit to memory. "But any teacher does more than engage in public discussion and instruction. There is also more informal teaching which takes place in private."[5] It may be that John has given us some of Jesus' informal discussions with His disciples and other people He met.

These are just a few of the differences between John and the other Gospels. In His wisdom, God has given us a fuller portrait of His Son than one human mind could convey.

Misunderstandings

In your first reading of John, you may have noticed that almost everyone who encounters Jesus in this Gospel misunderstands what He says and does. This fact and 20:31 suggest to some scholars that John wanted to clear up misunderstandings of what "the Christ" and "the Son of God" meant. The Jews had a distorted idea of the Messiah, so they were confused about Jesus' identity and mission. Even the disciples didn't understand Jesus' words and deeds until after the Resurrection, when Jesus and the Spirit began to make things clear (2:22, 7:39, 12:16, 16:13-16). From the time of Jesus onward, it was dangerous for a Jew to profess faith in Jesus (9:22,34; 12:42; 16:1-4; 19:38), and John may have wanted to encourage his fellow Jews to understand and believe in Jesus despite opposition.[6]

But John was not only trying to sort things out for Jewish converts. His Gospel so often explains Jewish customs that he seems to have had his eye on a Gentile audience as well. By the time John was writing, most Jews were rejecting the Gospel, but Christians were finding many Gentiles hungry for it. John was apparently as concerned that they believe accurately and actively as he was that Jewish converts do so.[7]

A pattern occurs over and over in John's Gospel. Jesus reveals something about Himself through a sign or some teaching, and people react in mixed ways. Some accept the revelation—these receive further revelation and have their misunderstandings clarified. Others reject the revelation, and their misunderstanding deepens. John 9:39 is Jesus' own statement on this pattern. As you study this Gospel, think about why John may have emphasized this pattern and what its implications are for you today.

15

Outline

Question 4 gave you a start on outlining John's Gospel. Many good and different outlines have been made of it, so you should feel free to make your own or look at some commentaries and Bible handbooks. As a broad framework, consider the following:

THE WITNESS TO JESUS
  I. Prologue (1:1-18)
  II. Public Ministry—Signs and Discourses (1:19-12:50)
  III. Private Ministry—Discourses for the Disciples (13:1-17:26)
  IV. The Passion[8]—The Great Sign (18:1-19:42)
  V. Resurrection Appearances—Signs (20:1-21:25)

As you study further, think about how you could improve these divisions and titles.

For the group

This "For the group" section and the ones in later lessons are intended to suggest ways of structuring your discussions. Feel free to select and adapt what suits your group. The main goals are to get to know John's Gospel as a whole and the people with whom you are going to study it.

Worship. Most groups like to begin with some kind of worship—a few minutes of prayer and/or a couple of songs. Worship helps people lay aside the business of the day and focus on God. It relaxes, renews, and opens you to listen to the Lord and each other. If you don't already have worship built into your meetings in some way, discuss how you might do so.

Warm-up. The beginning of a new study is a good time to lay a foundation for honest sharing of ideas, to get comfortable with each other, and to encourage a sense of common purpose. One way to establish common ground is to talk about what each group member hopes to get out of your group—out of any prayer, singing, sharing, outreach, or anything else you might do together. Why do you want to study the Gospel of John? What do you hope to give as well as receive? If you have someone write down each member's hopes and expectations, then you can look back at these goals later to see if they are being met. Goal-setting at the beginning can also help you avoid confusion when one person thinks the main point of the group is to learn the Scriptures, while another thinks it is to support each other in daily Christian life, and another thinks prayer or outreach is the chief business.

How to use this study. If the group has never used a LIFECHANGE study guide before, you might take a whole meeting to discuss your goals for the group and go over the "How to Use This Study" section on pages 5-8. Then you can take a second meeting to talk about the background and questions in this lesson. This will give you more time to read John and prepare lesson one for discussion.

Go over important points of the "How to Use This Study" section that you think the group should especially notice. For example, point out the optional questions in the margins. These are available as group discussion questions, ideas for application, and suggestions for further study. It is unlikely that anyone will have the time or desire to answer all the optional questions and do all the applications. A person might do one "Optional Application" for any given lesson. You might choose one or two "For Thought and Discussions" for your group discussion, or you might spend all your time on the numbered questions. If someone wants to write answers to the optional questions, suggest that he use a separate notebook. It will also be helpful for discussion notes, prayer requests, answers to prayers, application plans, and so on.

Invite everyone to ask questions about the "How to Use This Study" section.

Reading aloud. It is often helpful to refresh everyone's memory by reading aloud the passage you are going to study. You probably won't want to read all of John, but consider having someone read 1:1-18, another read 3:16-21, another 19:16-30, and another 20:1-9,19-23. These selections will remind the group of John's themes, his style, and his personality. You can shorten them if your time is limited.

First impressions. Ask the group to share first impressions of John's Gospel—its style, mood, content, or whatever strikes you. For instance, how is this book like and unlike the biographies people write today, and like and unlike the other three Gospels?

Next, zero in on John's themes and purposes by discussing questions 2, 5, and 6. Try to state as succinctly as possible what the book is about.

You probably don't need to discuss the evidence for whether John did or didn't write this Gospel. Also, you probably don't have to take a lot of time to compare your broad outlines (question 4). Do allow time for the group to share questions (question 7) and areas for application (questions 8 and 9).

You will probably want to leave many of the group's questions about the book until later in your study; they may answer themselves if you are looking for answers. Point out the list of references on pages 211-215, and encourage members to bring questions to their pastors or other Christians they respect.

Wrap-up. The group leader should have read lesson two and its "For the group" section. At this point, he or she can give a short summary of what members can expect in that lesson and the coming meeting. This is a chance to whet everyone's appetite, assign any optional questions, omit or clarify any numbered questions, or forewarn members of any possible difficulties.

You might also encourage anyone who found the overview especially hard. Some people are better at seeing the big picture or the whole of a book than others. Some are best at analyzing a particular verse or paragraph, while others are strongest at seeing how a passage applies to our lives. Urge members to give thanks for their own and others' strengths, and to give and request help when needed. The group is a place to learn from each other. Later lessons will draw on the gifts of close analyzers as well as overviewers and appliers, practical as well as theoretical thinkers.

Worship. Some groups like to end with singing and/or prayer. This can include songs and prayers that respond to what you've learned from John, or prayers for specific needs of group members. Many people are shy about sharing personal needs or praying aloud in groups, especially before they know the other people well. If this is true of your group, then a song and/or some silent prayer, and a short closing prayer by the leader, might be an appropriate end. You could share requests and pray in pairs instead, if appropriate.

1. Leon Morris, *The Gospel According to John* (Grand Rapids, Michigan: William B. Eerdmans Publishing Company, 1971), page 7. (Hereafter cited as "Morris.")
2. Morris, page 7, quoting Sir Edwyn Hoskyns, *The Fourth Gospel*, edited by F. N. Davey (London, 1947), page 20.
3. For an introduction, see Morris, pages 8-64; Raymond E. Brown, *The Gospel According to John (I-XII)*, The Anchor Bible, Volume 29 (New York: Doubleday and Company, 1966), pages xxiv-li, lxxx-civ; Leon Morris, *Studies in the Fourth Gospel* (Grand Rapids, Michigan: William B. Eerdmans Publishing Company, 1969), pages 139-292.
4. Morris, pages 30-35.
5. Morris, page 47.
6. John Painter, *John: Witness and Theologian* (London: SPCK, 1975), pages 12-15.
7. Ironically, his book was often misunderstood because he used Jewish symbols (word, light, darkness, truth, water) that had different meanings among Gentiles. Heretical groups used John's Gospel to prove their doctrines by misinterpreting the Jewish concepts.
8. Jesus' trial, torture, and death are called His Passion from the Latin word *passio*, "to suffer."

JOHN 1:1-18

The Word

Matthew and Luke begin their Gospels with Jesus' birth. Mark begins with His baptism. As you look at John's opening words, notice how different his starting place is.

Ask God to speak to you personally through your study of this passage and to help you hear it as though you have never heard it before. Then read 1:1-18 aloud with meaning in your voice. Listen to the words as you read them (this helps you take in the words with two senses at once). After that, reread the passage silently one or more times, possibly in different translations to get different flavors. Reading and rereading is the best way to observe what God is saying.

> **Study Skill—Observation**
> Sound interpretation of a passage is based on thorough observation of what it says. Observation is exciting if you approach a passage as though for the first time with all the old and new questions you can think of.
> Repetition is a major feature of John's style. Throughout his book, observe the words he considers important enough to repeat.

1. Write down everything 1:1-18 says about the Word.

   who or what He is _____

   _____

For Thought and Discussion: Why do you think John chose to begin his Gospel with the opening words of the creation account in Genesis?

_____

_____

_____

_____

_____

_____

_____

_____

_____

what He does _____

_____

_____

_____

_____

_____

_____

_____

In the beginning (1:1). The Jews of John's day called the book of Genesis "In the Beginning" because Genesis begins with these words. The Greek phrase can mean the moment of beginning (of history) or the root cause (of everything). John's Gospel is full of phrases that can have more than one meaning.[1]

Word (1:1). The Greek word *Logos* had rich associations for Jews and Greeks alike. Basically, it meant the reason or thought within a person, or the expression of his thought in speech. To a Jew, the *Logos* was the Word by which God spoke the universe into existence (Genesis 1:3,6,9; Psalm 33:6), by which He guided the prophets (Amos 1:3,6,9,11,13), by which He delivered His people (Psalm 107:19-20), and by which He accomplished His will (Isaiah 55:11). God's Word was potent and active. Also, when Jews paraphrased the Hebrew Scriptures into the languages the people spoke, they often substituted "the Word of God" for God's Name, which was considered too holy to utter.

Further, Jews began to use *Logos* for God's written Word of self-revelation in the Law. "Word," "Law," and "Wisdom" all referred to the agency by which God created and revealed Himself.

In Greek philosophy, the *Logos* was the eternal, impersonal Reason that pervaded and directed the universe. Gentiles might not have perceived John's Jewish sense of *Logos*, but they would have caught a glimpse.

For Thought and Discussion: What was the Father's role in creation? What was the Son's role? (See Genesis 1:1-3, John 1:3, 1 Corinthians 8:6.) Explain in your own words.

For Thought and Discussion: How can the Word both *be with* God and *be* God (1:1)?

Study Skill—Interpreting Terms

To understand the rich terms a writer uses, such as Word, light, world, and so on, you will often find it helpful to research cross-references to other parts of the New and Old Testaments and historical background about Greek or Jewish culture. You can find this information by:

1. looking up all the references to "word" in a concordance (see page 212);

2. looking up "word" in a Bible dictionary or Bible encyclopedia;

3. reading the cross-references in your study Bible.

2. John holds us in suspense about the Word's identity until 1:17. What do you think he means to imply about this Person by calling Him "the Word"?

For Further Study:
John uses the word
life (1:4) thirty-six
times, far more than
the other Gospels.
Watch for it as you
study. You might use
a concordance to find
all the references to
"life" in John's
Gospel.

_____

_____

_____

_____

_____

_____

Understood (1:5). This Greek word means basically
"to lay hold of so as to possess." It is normally
used to mean "to apprehend, to understand."
However, it can also mean "to overcome" or
"to overtake" (as in 12:35).[2] Again we find John
implying a double meaning.

3. Light and darkness are major symbols in John's
Gospel. What do they refer to and symbolize in
the Bible? (Consider some of the following:
Psalm 36:9; 82:5; 119:105,130; Proverbs 4:19;
Isaiah 60:1-2; John 3:19-21; Acts 26:18; Romans
13:12-14; Ephesians 5:8-14.)

light _____

_____

_____

_____

darkness _____

_____

_____

_____

4. Therefore, what does it imply about Jesus to call
Him the light (John 1:4-5,9; 8:12)?

_____

_____

22

_____

_____

_____

World (1:9). *Kosmos* is a key word in John's writings. Its root meaning is "order," the opposite of chaos. It also means "ornament" (as in 1 Peter 3:3), and it gives us our word "cosmetic." From there it came to be used for:

1. the universe, the greatest ordered ornament;
2. the physical earth;
3. the majority of people;
4. the human world order—social, economic, political, and religious systems;
5. the people and systems "hostile to Christ and all that He stands for."[3]

In this last sense, the world is corrupted by sin, so it is evil, dangerous, futile, temporary. Satan dominates the world (John 12:31, 1 John 5:19), that is, the world of people who are not yet born of God and freed from darkness. The world that God created to be a lovely and ordered ornament became an ugly and strife-torn world order because men rejected God and fell under the control of evil.

However, God loves the world of men and sent His Son to save it (3:16, 4:42, 6:51). God means to rescue the world (of helpless people) from the world (enslaved by Satan's system and men's own wickedness).

Thus, "world" has many shades of meaning, and John shifts from one to another without warning or uses the word in several senses at once. When you see it in a given passage, think carefully about what it means there.

Believed in his name (1:12). To the ancients, someone's name represented the essence of his character. To believe "on the name" (literally) of the Word means to trust who the Word really is. "It is not believing that what He says is true, but trusting Him as a person."[4] In Greek accounting documents, "on the name of" has the sense of

23

For Thought and Discussion: Compare 1:1 to 1:14. What is the Word's essential nature in each verse? Who is the Word "with" in each verse? What is astounding about this transition?

For Further Study: Watch for the words *glory* and *glorified* in John's Gospel. Observe how Jesus reveals His glory not just after the Resurrection, but throughout His ministry and especially on the Cross.

"to the possession of." So, John may also be saying that believing means yielding ourselves to be owned by Him whom we believe in.[5]

Glory (1:14). In the Old Testament, God's glory "is a *visible* manifestation of His majesty in *acts of power*"—a thunderstorm, a miracle, the cloud of fire that led Israel through the desert (Exodus 16:7-10, 24:17).[6]

Made his dwelling among us (1:14). The Greek verb means "to pitch one's tent," and the related noun means "tent" or "tabernacle." When Israel wandered in the wilderness, God's glory was present like a glowing cloud in "the Tabernacle," or "the Tent of Meeting" (Exodus 40:34-38). The rabbis came to call the glory in the Tabernacle (or Temple) the *Shekinah*, which means "[Someone or Something] dwelling"—that is, God dwelling among His people. Thus, when John says, **We have seen his glory** when He tented among us, he is boldly identifying the Word with the *Shekinah*: God visibly manifested in acts of power and dwelling among His people.[7]

But now the physical manifestation is not a fiery cloud: **The Word became flesh.** "Flesh" is here a crude, graphic word for physical humanness. It is a blunt way of ruling out any idea that the Word didn't become fully human.

Grace and truth (1:14). In the Greek Old Testament (the *Septuagint*), these words were used to translate an important pair of Hebrew words: *hesed* (lovingkindness, mercy, covenant love, steadfast love) and *emeth* (faithfulness, reliability, integrity, truth—Exodus 34:6; Psalms 85:10, 89:14). Grace and truth are primary traits of God. Grace is His unmerited favor and gifts for His creatures. But it is not a wishy-washy Santa Claus favor, for it harmonizes with God's truth—His integrity, His commitment to moral and factual reality. In fact, God is the only true reality, and everything else is measured by Him.[8]

Law (1:17). To the Jews, the Word of God and the Law of God were the same. They believed that the Word or Law or Wisdom of God existed before creation, was God's agent in creation, and was His agent in revealing Himself to people.[9] John insists that the Word, who is a Person, Jesus Christ, is different from and greater than the written Word or Law that Moses recorded. Yet, all that the Jews believed about the Law or Wisdom is really true of the Person who is the Word.

5. After you have taken an overview of a book, looking at its parts in depth will sharpen and even alter your understanding of why the whole was written. In your overview, you probably found that this book's purpose has to do with who Jesus is (20:31). On page 30 write down the main things 1:1-18 tells you about Jesus (who He is, what He came to do).

6. Think about what you observed in question 1 about who the Word is and what He does. Write down as many implications for your priorities, actions, and decisions as you can think of. For example, what difference does it make to you that Jesus . . .

is the Word? _____

_____

_____

_____

_____

is God? _____

_____

_____

_____

_____

was the means by which God created all things?

_____

_____

For Further Study:
a. "Grace" occurs in John's Gospel only in 1:14,16-17, but "truth" occurs twenty-five times and "true" twenty-three times.[10] Watch for what is said about truth, or do a word study with a concordance. Look for the meaning of truth and the source of truth. Why do you think John emphasizes truth?
b. Then, ask yourself how well your life reflects factual and moral truth. How can you live more fully by the truth?

For Thought and Discussion: Christians use the phrase "the Word of God" to refer to both Jesus and the Bible. In what sense are they both the *Logos*, and in what sense must we carefully distinguish between them?

For Further Study: Jesus used many symbols to describe Himself and the Holy Spirit that the Jews used to describe the Law—such as light, living water, and bread. Why do you think He did this?

For Thought and Discussion: In what sense is becoming a child of God a matter of a person's will (1:12)? In what sense is it a matter not of his will but of God's (1:13)?

For Thought and Discussion: What does 1:1-18 say about the human race's predicament and behavior?

_____

_____

_____

became flesh and dwelt among us? _____

_____

_____

_____

_____

gives certain people the right to become God's children?

_____

_____

_____

_____

_____

_____

other _____

_____

_____

_____

_____

_____

_____

_____

Study Skill—Application
Bible study should not be merely gathering information. Keep your study exciting by making your discoveries about God into opportu-
(continued on page 27)

(continued from page 26)
nities for worship. Take a few moments right now to reflect on what you have observed about Jesus. Praise Him for who He is and what He has done. Ask Him to make the implications of these truths more real to you. Also, ask Him to enable you to act on these implications.

7. What can you do this week by God's grace to let one truth from question 6 more fully affect your character and habits? (Be as specific as possible about the prayer and other action you want to pursue.)

_____

_____

_____

_____

_____

_____

Study Skill—Questions

It is a good habit, whenever you have a question, to write it down immediately. These questions are sometimes routine, but they sometimes point you to a truth that God wants to bring alive for you. It pays to review your questions to see if God's Spirit is prompting you through them.

8. If you have any questions about 1:1-18, write them down so that you can look for answers.

_____

_____

_____

_____

_____

Optional Application: Take five minutes each day for the next week to ponder one of the truths John states about the Word. Praise God for this truth, and thank Him for how it affects you.

a. For example, thank God for giving you the light of Jesus to understand the world and to know what is right and wrong. Thank Him for the fact that darkness has neither understood nor overcome Jesus' light. Ask Him to help you live by that light in your particular circumstances and trust Him to enable you to resist the weight of darkness.

b. Or, thank the eternal Word for lowering Himself to become fully human with physical flesh, and for living among us. Thank Him for putting up with all the limitations of flesh and even enduring the rejection of the people He created and loved. Ask Him to help you respond to His generosity with the active, committed faith He desires.

For the group

Worship.

Warm-up. People often come to Bible studies with their minds full of the day's business. Worship helps them shift gears. Another help is to begin with a simple question that deals with the topic of the study but focuses on personal experience. This also helps group members come to understand each other better so that they become more free to share their struggles and joys in living by God's Word.

A possible warm-up for this lesson is, "What does a word do?"

Read aloud. Even when the group has studied a passage ahead of time, most people will be glad to have their memories refreshed. So, have someone read 1:1-18 aloud slowly.

Summarize. Before you examine the details of this passage, step back and consider what the whole of it is about. Ask one or two people to summarize the passage in a sentence or two. Don't expect a perfect summary at this stage; this is just a place from which to begin.

Questions. Start by letting everyone list as many observations for question 1 as possible. It might be helpful to write them all on a large piece of paper for everyone to see. Then examine some of the things John says about the Word one by one. Discuss first what a statement (such as that He is the Word, that He is with God and is God, that in Him is life, that He became flesh) means—this is interpretation. Then discuss what difference this fact makes to you—this is the beginning of application. You probably won't have time to examine everything John says in detail, so choose two to five statements that seem most significant.

When you've discussed each one, give everyone a chance to share how he or she wants to act on something in the passage. Encourage everyone to commit to some application, even if it is only to worship Christ for some aspect of His nature every day this week. You don't want to suggest that group members must do something to earn God's approval, but you do want to encourage them to grow in relationship with and obedience to God.

28

This lesson is full of background material because the prologue introduces several terms that are keys in this Gospel. Advise the group that it is not necessary to absorb every detail of the background. It is there to help you, not overwhelm you. Ignore any of it if necessary.

Summarize. Summarize what you've learned from 1:1-18 and how you plan to respond.

Wrap-up. This lesson skipped over 1:6-8 because lesson three deals with the testimony of John the Baptist in that paragraph as well as 1:19-34 and 3:22-36. Explain this if necessary.

Also, plan to begin your next meeting by letting each person share how his or her efforts to apply something in 1:1-18 went. Don't give the impression that everyone must report some measurable transformation. This is simply a chance for members to share frustrations, insights, and questions about applying this passage. You can help each other overcome obstacles to taking time for prayer or active application, rejoice with each other over new attitudes about a situation, and learn from each other's discoveries.

Worship. John 1:1-18 is almost a hymn about Jesus. Use it as a springboard to praise by taking turns praising Jesus for what John says about Him. Thank Him for who He is and what He has done for you.

1. Morris, page 73.
2. Morris, pages 85-86.
3. Morris, page 127.
4. Morris, page 99.
5. Morris, pages 99-100.
6. Brown, volume 29, pages 503-504.
7. Morris, pages 103-104.
8. Morris, page 294.
9. Painter, page 25.
10. There are actually two words for "true" in John's Gospel. See Brown, volume 29, page 499.

Jesus' Identity

JOHN 1:6-8,19-51

Testimony

When John the Baptist began his ministry, he was
Israel's first prophet in four hundred years. He was
known throughout Palestine, adored by the crowds,
grudgingly respected by the religious leaders, and
feared by the secular authorities. Even decades after
his death, disciples of his could be found in cities as
far away as Ephesus (Acts 18:24-25, 19:1-7). He was
much more unanimously acclaimed and long
remembered by the Jews than Jesus was. Probably
for this reason, John the Apostle begins his book of
evidence about Jesus with the Baptist's testimony.[1]

Read 1:6-8,19-51, carefully observing what is
revealed about John and Jesus. Try to put yourself
into the characters' places. Ask yourself how they
would have been feeling while the events were
going on. This technique may help you involve
yourself more personally in the narrative.

The Baptist's testimony (1:6-8,19-34)

John the Apostle never names himself in his Gospel;
the name "John" always refers to John the Baptist.
When there is a chance of confusion, we will call
the former "the Evangelist" (a person who writes an
evangel or Gospel) and the latter "the Baptist."

1. Who or what did the Baptist say he was
   (1:6-8,19-34)? How did he describe himself?

_____

_____

_____

_____

_____

2. What did the Baptist testify about Jesus? Record as many observations as you can find.

_____

_____

_____

_____

_____

_____

3. How would you describe John the Baptist's mission in your own words?

_____

_____

_____

_____

_____

_____

The Christ (1:20). Greek for "the Anointed One," a translation of the Hebrew word *Messiah*. In Old Testament times "various people were anointed, but notably priests and kings. . . . The rite was used to set men apart for special functions. When in due course the expectation grew up that one day God would send into the world an especially great Person, a mighty Deliverer, One who would represent Him in a very special sense, this coming great One was thought of not as 'an anointed', but as *the* anointed one', *'the* Messiah'."[2]

At the time the Baptist appeared, the Jews were fervently looking for the Messiah. Different groups had widely different ideas of what He might be like. Most Jews expected that His appearance would herald the last days and that He would be a military leader to regain political control of Palestine. John's Gospel shows a lot about what the Jews did and didn't expect from their Messiah.

Elijah (1:21). The prophet Elijah did not die but was taken up into heaven (2 Kings 2:11). The later prophet Malachi foretold that "before that great and terrible day of the LORD," God would send Elijah back to earth (Malachi 4:5). The Jews thought this meant he would come just before the Messiah.

Jesus said that the Baptist was "the Elijah who was to come" (Matthew 11:14), but the Baptist did not perceive himself this way. The Jews expected the identical person who had lived almost nine hundred years earlier, and the Baptist knew he wasn't that man. Yet the Baptist ministered "in the spirit and power of Elijah" (Luke 1:17).

The Prophet (1:21). Before the coming of the Messiah, the Jews also expected the prophet like Moses described in Deuteronomy 18:15-22.

Pharisees (1:24). The name meant "the separated ones." They separated themselves from lax religious practices and lived strictly by the Law. In order to avoid breaking the Law, they had minutely defined the precise ways each law must be kept in every conceivable situation. Most of the aristocrats and chief priests belonged to the party of the Sadducees, who stressed Temple worship, opposed the detailed expansion of the Law, and had political control of the nation with Roman support. By contrast, the Pharisees represented the common people interested in religion untainted by politics. They were the real moral and doctrinal force among the Jewish people. Some Pharisees loved God, but the emphasis on rules encouraged spiritual pride and external religion. Many

For Further Study:
a. For more on the Baptist's mission and message, see Luke 1:13-17,76-80; 3:1-18.

b. Compare John 1:32-34 to Matthew 3:13-17.

c. See the full passage the Baptist mentions in John 1:23—Isaiah 40:3-11.

For Thought and Discussion: How did Jesus take away the sins of the world like a sacrificial lamb? See John 19:17-30, Romans 3:21-26, Hebrews 9:1-10:18.

For Thought and Discussion: a. The Jewish sect at Qumran believed they had to prepare themselves for the Lord's coming, but they felt no responsibility to prepare others. Is this how John the Baptist looked at preparing and making the way straight? Explain.
b. How are you called to prepare for the Lord's coming? How are you doing this? How can you improve in this area?

Pharisees considered themselves the experts on God's system, which was too complicated for an ordinary person to grasp, let alone keep. Therefore, if a man was preaching and baptizing, it was their job to know exactly what he was doing and why.

Baptize (1:25-26,33). When people converted to Judaism, the males were circumcised and both sexes were baptized. The rite washed away the pollution of the Gentile world. John was shocking the nation by insisting that born-and-bred Jews also needed cleansing. Based on Ezekiel 36:25 and Zechariah 13:1, some Jews expected that all would be baptized when the time of the Messiah came, but John denied being the Messiah. The Pharisees wanted an explanation.[3]

Sandals (1:27). Disciples did not pay for their teachers' wisdom, but they were expected to perform many services for them. However, they drew the line at extremely menial tasks like loosing the teacher's sandal thong. That was slave's work, and the rabbis were forbidden to expect it of their disciples. But the Baptist declared himself unworthy to perform even this most menial service for the One who was coming.[4]

The Lamb of God (1:29,35). This phrase was not in use among the Jews for anything. Apparently, it originated with John the Baptist and was rarely used until John the Evangelist wrote it down. It was not an obvious reference to the Passover sacrifice (which was called "the Passover" and might be a kid or a lamb), nor to the lamb in Isaiah 53:7 (which the Jews did not think was about the Messiah), nor to any other particular lamb. It seems that God revealed to the Baptist that the Messiah would be the fulfillment of the whole Jewish sacrificial system, from the daily offerings to the yearly Passover. The Baptist was inspired to coin the term "Lamb of God" to explain this to his disciples.[5]

4. Why is it important to you personally that Jesus is the Lamb of God?

34

_____

_____

_____

_____

For Further Study:
Using a concordance, research the implications of "lamb." Start with Genesis 22:8.

Five disciples (1:35-51)

Disciples (1:35). "'Learners' . . . those who had attached themselves to a given teacher."[6] This was a relationship of personal commitment and submission, like father and son. Teachers and disciples expected utter loyalty from each other. To let a disciple follow another teacher without a murmur was extraordinary.

Andrew was one of the Baptist's disciples. The other is unnamed, but tradition has it that he was the Evangelist.

---

5. What did each of the following discover about Jesus, and how did each discover this?

Andrew and the other disciple (1:35-41) _____

_____

_____

_____

Andrew's brother Simon (1:40-42) _____

_____

_____

_____

Philip (1:43-45) _____

_____

For Thought and Discussion: a. In what ways are Andrew, Philip, and Nathanael like and unlike yourself after being newly introduced to Jesus?
b. What can you learn for your own life from their example?

For Thought and Discussion: What do you think was the significance of Simon's new name "little rock" (1:42)?

Nathanael (1:45-50) _____

_____

_____

_____

_____

6. How would you describe Jesus from what He says and does in 1:37-39,42-43,47-51? What impressions do you get of Him?

_____

_____

_____

_____

_____

_____

_____

The Son of Man (1:51). This is the Aramaic way of saying "man" or "the man." It was Jesus' favorite way of referring to Himself, but John 12:34 suggests that it was not a familiar term for the Messiah.

The term probably came from Daniel 7:13-14, where it refers to a heavenly person. Also, God called Ezekiel "son of man" and commanded him to bear the sin of Israel and Judah in a symbolic affliction (Ezekiel 4:1-5:17). "Son of Man" was a good choice for Jesus because it did not have the distorted political implications of "Messiah."

7. What do you think Jesus is implying about Himself in 1:51?

_____

_____

_____

_____

_____

_____

For Thought and Discussion: In 1:51, Jesus is referring to Jacob's dream in Genesis 28:10-12. What is Jesus saying about Himself by comparing Himself to a staircase between heaven and earth?

8. What apparently convinces Andrew, Philip, and Nathanael that Jesus is the Messiah and the Son of God?

_____

_____

_____

_____

For Thought and Discussion: a. Why do you think Jesus said what He did to Nathanael in 1:50-51?

b. How might you have felt if you had been Nathanael hearing these words?

9. From 1:50-51, does it seem that Jesus is satisfied with their level of understanding and belief? Why do you think He is or isn't?

_____

_____

_____

_____

_____

Your response

10. On page 30, write down what 1:19-51 reveals about who Jesus is.

11. Think about the Baptist's and the disciples' testimony about Jesus, and about what convinced each of them. Also, reflect on what each of

37

Optional Application: Take time to praise Jesus for being the Messiah, the Lamb of God, the Son of God, the King of Israel, or something else revealed about Him in 1:19-51.

Optional Application: Are you following Jesus as a disciple (1:37,43)? How is this affecting your actions? How should it affect them?

Optional Application: "Come and see," said Jesus and Philip (1:39,46). How can you invite someone to come and see Jesus?

them did about what they heard and believed.

What implications does their example have for your life?

_____

_____

_____

_____

_____

_____

12. What do you think you should do about this testimony this week? Be as specific as possible.

_____

_____

_____

_____

_____

_____

13. List any questions you have about 1:6-8,19-51.

_____

_____

_____

_____

_____

For the group

Warm-up. Ask each person to share very briefly how he or she was first introduced to Jesus. This should not be a complete testimony, but a short sketch of who and how and when the first introduction—not necessarily the final conversion or commitment—occurred.

Read aloud and summarize.

The Baptist's testimony. Questions 1 and 2 are observations. Let the group list as many descriptions of John as it can, then discuss what the descriptions mean and summarize the Baptist's mission. Likewise, let the group list descriptions of Jesus, then interpret each one and summarize the whole. Next, examine how one or two (such as "the Lamb of God") apply to you.

Five disciples. Again, the focus here is on what you can learn about Jesus from this passage, and how you can each respond to the testimony with action. Help each other plan applications that include prayer, reliance on God, and action.

Wrap-up.

Worship. The titles given Jesus in this passage are ideal springboards to worship. Praise Him for being the Lamb of God, the Son of God, the Son of Man, the staircase between heaven and earth, the One whose sandal you are unworthy to loose, the King of Israel.

1. Morris, page 87-88.
2. Morris, page 134.
3. Morris, page 140.
4. Morris, page 141.
5. Morris, pages 143-148.
6. Morris, page 155.

JOHN 2:1-25

The Ministry Begins

On the first five days of His ministry, Jesus began to gather some key disciples from among the Baptist's followers (1:19-51). With them, He has gone to Galilee. What will be the Word's first works as He begins His mission? Read 2:1-25.

Water to wine (2:1-11)

Wedding (2:1). The bridegroom and his friends brought the bride to the groom's house in a torchlit procession. Then there was a wedding feast that could last as long as a week.[1]

   In the Old Testament, the wedding symbolizes the time of the Messiah (Isaiah 54:4-8, 62:4-5), when God will again marry His Bride, Israel.

No more wine (2:3). Hospitality and weddings in particular were taken extremely seriously in the Near East. To fail in hospitality was a dark blot on the family's reputation. Even if they were poor and hoping to manage with the minimum of expenses, they were in trouble. "[I]t was possible to take legal action in certain circumstances against a man who had failed to provide the appropriate wedding gift . . . [so] when the supply of wine failed more than social embarrassment was involved." The bridegroom and his family were open to being fined heavily.[2]

For Thought and Discussion: Among the Greeks there was a myth that the god Dionysus turned water into wine. This was a Greek way of saying that rain fell on the vines, they produced grapes, then men bottled the grape juice, and in some mysterious way the juice became wine. To the Greeks, this annual process was a miracle of the divine forces of Nature. How do you think John's Greek readers would have responded to a story of Jesus turning water into wine in a matter of seconds?

41

For Further Study:
Use a concordance to
find "wedding" and
"bridegroom" in the
New Testament.

For Further Study:
Jesus' "time" (2:4) is
a recurring theme in
John's Gospel. Exam-
ine each reference,
and trace the pattern
you find. What is
Jesus' "time" or
"hour" (7:6,8,30;
8:20; 12:23,27;
13:1; 16:32; 17:1).

**For Thought and
Discussion:** How is it
significant that Jesus
chose to turn the Jew-
ish water of purifica-
tion into wine for a
wedding banquet?

Furthermore, wine was a symbol of joy. It was drunk well-diluted with water to avoid carousing, but it was essential at a joyous occasion like a wedding feast. Without this crucial symbol, the banquet would be spoiled.[3]

In the Old Testament, wine is a central part of the messianic wedding banquet (Isaiah 25:6). An abundance of wine also symbolizes the joy of the last days (Jeremiah 31:12, Amos 9:13-14).

Six stone water jars (2:6). Daily life, especially contact with Gentiles and the secular world, made a Jew ceremonially unclean or unholy (Mark 7:3-4). Therefore, Jews poured water over their hands before eating, studying the Law, and so on. A lot of water was necessary for many guests, so this household had jars with a total capacity of more than 120 gallons.

Signs (2:11). John prefers this word for Jesus' miracles. As opposed to words that stress the miraculousness or the power of Jesus' deeds, a *sign* is something that points beyond itself. It teaches a spiritual truth; it points to God and His provision in Jesus. In each of Jesus' signs, He shows Himself to be sufficient in some facet of human need in which people are inadequate. He shows Himself to be the Son of God doing the works of God.

The signs are like parables acted out. Each one demonstrates an aspect of Jesus' mission. They reveal what God is like. They illustrate and prove Jesus' claims about Himself (that He is the light of the world, the source of life, etc.). They are meant to produce faith. But they don't compel faith, for like the parables, they can be ignored or misunderstood.[4]

John 2:1-12:50 has been called "The Book of Signs"[5] because in these chapters John records a few carefully selected signs that reveal Jesus' identity. The ultimate sign, of course, is the Crucifixion and Resurrection. (See 12:37, 20:30-31.)

1. How did Jesus' first sign affect His disciples (2:11)?

_____

_____

_____

_____

2. Think about the purpose of a sign. What does this particular sign reveal about Jesus' character, identity, and mission?

_____

_____

_____

_____

_____

_____

_____

3. What does Jesus' first sign reveal about His Father's character and values?

_____

_____

_____

_____

_____

_____

4. If you wanted a cross-reference for 2:1-11, you could look up "wine" in a concordance. This could lead you to Luke 5:37-39, where Jesus speaks about new wine and old wineskins. What parallel truths can you see in these two passages?

_____

_____

_____

For Further Study: Compare John 2:1-11 to Luke 5:33-35 and 7:33-35. What do these passages all reveal about Jesus' personality and approach to life?

For Thought and Discussion: Why do you suppose Jesus made more than 120 gallons of wine—far more than the family could use in months?

For Thought and Discussion: Why do you think Jesus chose turning water into wine for a wedding as His first sign? (Think of as many reasons as possible.)

**Optional
Application:** How is
the miracle of chang-
ing dirty water into
wedding wine signifi-
cant for you?

**Optional
Application:** Does
2:13-17 have any
warnings about Chris-
tians' priorities? If so,
how do these relate
to you? What do you
think Jesus would say
and do if He arrived in
your church, fellow-
ship, or family?

_____

_____

_____

5. How are these truths applicable to your life?

_____

_____

_____

_____

_____

Cleansing the Temple (2:12-25)

Passover (2:13). Exodus 12 explains this feast. It
was one of the annual feasts that all male Jews
were supposed to celebrate in Jerusalem (Deuteronomy 16:16).

Temple (2:14). In order to satisfy his passion for
building and win the favor of his subjects,
Herod the Great had undertaken to build a
magnificent Temple. The project was begun in
19 BC and not finished until 64 AD.[6] Although it
was only half-done when Jesus was there, it was
breathtaking and in full operation.

The Temple proper (the Holy Place) was
surrounded by several courts. The innermost
court was open only to Jewish men, the next
admitted both Jewish men and women, and the
outermost admitted Gentiles as well as Jews.
The Court of the Gentiles was huge—some five
hundred by three hundred yards—and it was
here that Jesus probably *found men selling cat-
tle, sheep and doves, and others sitting at
tables exchanging money.*

These businesses were essential to the
sacrificial system. People who came from
hundreds of miles away could hardly bring
animals with them, so they needed to buy them
in Jerusalem. Also, since one was allowed to
give money to the temple treasury only in

Tyrian coinage, there had to be someone who could exchange Greek, Roman, or other coins for the acceptable type. However, there was no reason why these transactions could not have taken place near but outside the Temple. The Court of the Gentiles was supposed to be the place where Gentiles could meet and worship the true God. The marketplace bedlam would have made this impossible.[7]

My Father's house (2:16). A Jew might speak of "my Father in heaven" or "our Father in heaven," but never of "my Father." But Jesus often referred to God in this shockingly familiar way.[8]

6. What do Jesus' words and deeds in 2:13-17 tell you about His character and priorities? What do they tell you about His mission?

_____

_____

_____

_____

_____

_____

7. How was Jesus going to prove His authority to throw the vendors out of the Temple (2:18-22)?

_____

_____

_____

_____

8. What do these two paragraphs tell you about Jesus?

2:18-22 _____

For Thought and Discussion: Why do you think Jesus felt so strongly about the vendors? (*Optional:* Compare Mark 11:15-17.)

For Further Study: Compare John 2:12-25 to Matthew 21:12-13, Mark 11:15-17, and Luke 19:45-46. How were the circumstances of the cleansing at the beginning of Jesus' ministry like and unlike those of the one at the end of His ministry?

45

_____

_____

_____

_____

2:23-25 _____

_____

_____

_____

Your response

9. On page 30, summarize what you learned about Jesus from chapter 2. Use questions 2, 6, and 8 to help you.

10. What insight from 2:1-25 seems most signifi-cant to you personally?

_____

_____

_____

_____

_____

11. How would you like this truth to affect your life?

_____

_____

_____

_____

12. What steps can you take this week to begin let-ting this happen?

_____

_____

_____

_____

_____

13. List any questions you have about 2:1-25.

_____

_____

_____

For the group

Warm-up. Ask, "Do you think of Jesus as interested more in love and joy or more in justice and holiness?" Let everyone answer. When the group summarizes 2:1-25, point out that this chapter shows both sides of Him—making wine for a wedding and throwing vendors out of His Father's house.

Read aloud and summarize. Briefly, what happens in 2:1-25?

Water into wine. Each time you interpret a sign, as in 2:1-11, it will be important to remember the meaning of a *sign*, explained on page 42. Help the group see how the miracle was a sign, not just a work of power. Jesus chose His signs carefully, and John selected just a few to include in his Gospel, so each one has a specific message that we should not miss. Here are some questions to consider: What does the sign point to about Jesus? The Father? God's Kingdom? Don't forget to discuss how this sign is relevant to you.

Cleansing the Temple. Although this was not a miracle, it was a sign in the sense that it was an active parable of Jesus' mission. The questions focus on what the scene reveals about Jesus.

Worship. Praise Jesus for being the One who turns water into wine, who transforms human religion into a Kingdom of abundant joy and celebration, who insists on the purity of His Father's house of worship, whose death and resurrection revealed Him as the true Temple that replaced the manmade one. Ask Him to help you take seriously His mission to transform your system into His Kingdom.

Chronology

John 1:19-2:11 seems to be the first week of Jesus' ministry:

    Day 1 (1:19-28)
    Day 2 ("The next day," 1:29-34)
    Day 3 ("The next day," 1:35-40)
    Day 4 (after the two disciples "spent that
        day" with Jesus, 1:41-42)
    Day 5 ("The next day," 1:43-51)
    Day 6 (travel to Galilee)
    Day 7 ("On the third day," 2:1-11)[9]

If this is accurate, then John 1:1-2:11 resembles Genesis 1:1-2:3. Like Genesis, John opens with "In the beginning" and proceeds to recount the first momentous week of a new creation. This time, the Word of God has become flesh and entered His handiwork to re-create it.

The timing or sequence of events often has significance for what the author is trying to accomplish. Learn to identify words or phrases that give you clues to the sequence of events.

---

1. Morris, page 178; Brown, volume 29, page 97.
2. Morris, page 177.
3. Morris, page 179.
4. Morris, pages 684-688.
5. Brown, volume 29, pages cxxxviii-cxliv.
6. Morris, page 200.
7. F. F. Bruce, *New Testament History* (New York: Doubleday and Company, 1971), pages 189-190.
8. Morris, page 195, note 66.
9. These are the divisions of days given in Morris, pages 129-130; and Brown, volume 29, pages 105-106. Brown adds some scholars' speculations of how Day 1 was a Wednesday and Day 7 was Tuesday night/Wednesday, since Jewish tradition required a virgin to be married on a Wednesday. See Brown, volume 29, pages 98, 106.

JOHN 3:1-36

Born of the Spirit

Having come to Jerusalem for the Passover, Jesus has won the undying hatred of the Sadducees, the party of the priests who control the Temple. By driving the merchants out of the Temple, Jesus has publicly denounced the way the Sadducees are treating God and His house. The other party of Jewish leaders, the Pharisees, may well be applauding this jab at men whom the Pharisees think are obsessed with power and temple rites at the expense of the other commandments. Thus, it isn't entirely surprising that a Pharisee would come to see if this small town firebrand's views accord with his own. But the learned leader is in for a surprise. Read 3:1-36.

Nicodemus and Jesus (3:1-21)

A member of the Jewish ruling council (3:1). The Sanhedrin, the body of seventy elders that controlled Jewish matters in Jerusalem and had great moral authority elsewhere in Palestine and even outside it. The Sanhedrin included both Sadducees and Pharisees.

As a leading Pharisee, Nicodemus was a spiritual and social leader. He was trained to believe that by obeying each technicality of God's Law, he was attaining God's approval and a place in what the Jews called the world or age to come. The common people might be ignorant about the fine points of God's commands, and

49

God would judge them for this. But Nicodemus certainly knew and lived the laws. Naturally there were areas in which he needed to improve, but by and large a leading Pharisee could be confident that his place in the world to come was secure. Yet, Nicodemus came to Jesus.

1. Given the circumstances in which Nicodemus chose to visit Jesus (3:2), what do you think Nicodemus's purpose was?

_____

_____

_____

_____

2. From Jesus' words in 3:3, what question do you think He saw in Nicodemus's heart? (*Optional:* Compare Luke 18:18.)

_____

_____

_____

_____

_____

Kingdom of God (3:3). This phrase occurs dozens of times in the Synoptic Gospels, but only here in John. It is one of Jesus' main themes. It sometimes means God's eternal kingship over the universe. At other times, Jesus says that the Kingdom is already present in the person of Jesus, the King. At still other times, He speaks of the Kingdom as not yet present—a spiritual or even physical reality that is yet to come. The already-but-not-yet and the spiritual-yet-very-real aspects of the Kingdom make it a rich term.

Born again (3:3). Another double meaning: the Greek phrase also means "born from above."

Born of water and the Spirit (3:5). Interpretations of this phrase include the following:

1. Water represents repentance and purification, as in John the Baptist's "baptism of repentance" (Mark 1:4). Indeed, Jesus was also having His disciples baptize (John 3:22, 4:1-2). Nicodemus needs to enter into all that the Baptist's purifying water symbolizes, and also to enter "the totally new divine life that Jesus would impart"[1] by the Spirit of God.

2. Water represents natural procreation—human semen (this was a common symbol in ancient times). Nicodemus must be born both naturally and "of the Spirit."

3. Water represents spiritual procreation. Nicodemus must be born of procreative water and Spirit, a Greek way of saying "spiritual seed"[2] or "the seed of the Spirit."

4. Water refers to Christian baptism. (This may have been a secondary understanding in the Evangelist's mind, but Jesus probably wasn't talking to Nicodemus about a rite that did not yet exist.)

Wind . . . Spirit (3:8). The Greek word *pneuma* means "spirit," "breath," and "wind." The breath of a person is or represents the principle of life in him; when he stops breathing, life is gone. Wind is like breath. God's Spirit is His breath (Genesis 2:7) and is like wind.[3]

---

3. In your own words, explain Jesus' answer to Nicodemus (3:3,5-8).

_____

_____

_____

_____

_____

_____

_____

For Thought and Discussion: How is it possible to be reborn (3:5-8)?

Optional Application: Have you been reborn from above? If so, how do you know? How has this affected your life? If not, what can you do about this?

For Thought and Discussion: a. What aspects of a person's life demonstrate that he or she has been transformed by the new birth?

b. To what extent does this happen all at once, and to what extent does it take time?

c. Use your own life as an example. How has the new birth transformed you? What areas of your life still need to be transformed by the Spirit?

For Thought and Discussion: How is God's Spirit like ordinary wind (3:8)?

For Thought and Discussion: What is Jesus saying in 3:10-12?

Optional Application: a. How is 3:1-15 a model for your evangelism? How can you present these truths in a way that your friends will understand them? Ask God about this.
b. Commit yourself to praying for one person you know to be reborn.

For Thought and Discussion: What are some ways in which you can tell that someone is depending on something other than new birth to enter God's Kingdom?

4. Why is new birth, not just a right mental belief and a godly lifestyle, necessary for seeing and entering God's Kingdom?

_____

_____

_____

_____

_____

_____

Son of Man (3:13). See note on 1:51 (page 36).

Lifted up (3:14). Another double meaning. The Greek means equally to exalt or to physically lift.[4] (Compare 12:23,32-33.)

Eternal (3:15). John prefers the term "eternal life" to "the Kingdom of God"—the two are equivalent in Jesus' teaching, but John emphasizes how Jesus' kingship was misunderstood. John uses "eternal" nearly three times as much as any other New Testament book. It means basically "pertaining to an age." The Jews divided time into this age and the age to come, and *aionios* referred to life in the one to come. Since life in the age to come will never end, *aionios* came to mean "everlasting" or "eternal."[5] Thus, the word implies a quantity (everlasting) as well as a quality (measureless, abundant, characteristic of God's Kingdom) of life.

5. Jesus had barely begun His ministry. But according to 3:14-15, what did Jesus already know about His mission?

_____

_____

_____

_____

_____

For Further Study:
On the snake in John
3:14, see Numbers
21:4-9.

Loved (3:16). John's Gospel has this verb (*agapao*)
thirty-six times and a similar verb (*phileo*) thirteen times, both more than twice as often as
any of the other three Gospels. John doesn't
seem to distinguish greatly between these two
verbs.[6] But *agapao* and the noun *agape* are the
words Greek-speaking Jews used to talk about
God's selfless, committed love for Israel. *Phileo*
and the noun *philia* emphasize God's warm
affection for His people, while *agape* is "a selfless, purposeful, outgoing attitude that desires
to do good to the one loved."[7] *Agape* stresses
the will somewhat more than the emotions; it is
a deliberate, free act of love. In any case, no
Jewish writer ever suggested that God loved *the
world* with either emotions or will.[8]

Gave (3:16). A double meaning. The Father first
gave His Son by sending Him into the world in
flesh, then gave Him up to death on the Cross.

_____

6. What does 3:16-18 tell us about . . .

God the Father? _____

_____

_____

_____

_____

_____

Jesus the Son? _____

_____

_____

_____

_____

**For Thought and
Discussion:** a. What
can we learn about
the Father from the
fact that He voluntar-
ily "gave" His own
Son for the corrupt
world of humans?
b. What does this
act reveal about the
meaning of love?

For Further Study:
Using a concordance,
study all that John's
Gospel has to say
about love.

**Optional
Application:** a. Medi-
tate this week on
what 3:16-17 tells
you about the Father.
Let this truth really
sink in as you pray
about it. What differ-
ence does (or should)
it make to your atti-
tudes and priorities?
b. Is there any
deep-rooted anger or
fear in you that
makes it hard for you
to fully believe this
truth about the
Father? If so, confess
this to God. You might
ask someone else to
pray with you about
this.

For Further Study:
John uses the verb
krino (to judge or
condemn) and the
related nouns thirty-
one times. Use a
concordance to find
them ("condemn,"
"condemnation,"
"judgment," "judge"),
and come to some
conclusions about
John's teaching on
judgment. Start with
3:17-18 and 9:39.

**For Thought and
Discussion:** Is it
possible to live by the
truth through one's
own moral effort?
Consider 3:3 and
3:21 carefully.

**Optional
Application:** Does
your behavior indicate
that you love dark-
ness or light? How
happy would you be if
God exposed all your
current habits and
practices to the light?
Pray about this. Does
anything in you need
to change? If so, what
and how?

> **Study Skill—Paraphrasing**
> Putting verses into your own words is an
> excellent way to explore and digest their
> meaning.

7. Describe in your own words the stark alternatives that face each person (3:18-21).

   _____

   _____

   _____

   _____

   _____

   _____

   _____

8. Jesus came because of God's love to save, not to
   condemn. Why, then, do most people hate Him
   (3:19-21)?

   _____

   _____

   _____

   _____

   _____

The Baptist testifies again (3:22-36)

9. In 3:30 the Baptist says, "He must become
   greater; I must become less." According to
   3:22-26, why was this necessary?

   _____

   _____

   _____

   _____

_____

_____

_____

**Optional
Application:** Does
the Baptist's attitude
toward himself and
his own ministry, and
toward Jesus and His
ministry, suggest any
example for you to
follow? Do your
actions reflect 3:30?
Pray about how you
can grow in this area.

10. In 1:35-37, the Baptist in effect sent his own
    disciples to follow Jesus instead. Later he
    explicitly put himself below Jesus (3:27-30).
    What does this tell you about John the Baptist?

_____

_____

_____

_____

Sent (3:28,34). The two verbs for "to send" (*apo-
stello* and *pempo*) occur a total of sixty times in
John's Gospel. Forty-one of these times refer to
the Father sending the Son. The words often
imply a special commission or a special relationship between the sender and the sent.
Behind this sense is the Jewish office of the
shaliach (from the Hebrew *shalach*, "to send").
He was "a person acting with full authority for
another,"[9] an ambassador or proxy. A *shaliach*
could stand in for either party in a betrothal or
deliver a certificate of divorce. A rabbi sent by
the Sanhedrin to inspect synagogues or collect
tithes was a *shaliach*. The rabbis said that "the
man sent by the man *is* the man."
    The delegation "sent" from the Sanhedrin
to the Baptist (1:19,22,24) may have been a
group of *shaluchim* in this official sense. The
Baptist was "sent" (3:28) by God for an official
mission. But Jesus was the Father's preeminent
shaliach, as Jesus stresses in 3:34; 5:24,30;
6:38,44,57; 7:16,29,33; 8:16,18,26,29. The *shaliach* did nothing on his own initiative, did
everything to please and serve his sender, and
had all authority from his sender.
    As Jesus is the Father's *shaliach*, so His
disciples are Jesus' *shaluchim* (13:20, 17:18,

20:21). The Greek translation of *shaliach* is *apostolos* or "apostle."

11. Reread 3:1-36, and write on page 30 what you learn about Jesus' identity from this chapter.

12. Now, summarize how 3:1-36 says we should respond to these truths about Jesus.

Your response

13. What one truth from this chapter would you like to take to heart and act upon?

---

14. How would you like this truth to affect your life?

---

15. What action can you take to begin letting this happen by God's grace?

_____

_____

_____

_____

_____

16. List any questions you have about chapter 3.

_____

_____

_____

_____

For the group

Warm-up. Ask, "What does being born imply to you? If you didn't already know about Christianity, what would you think of if someone told you you needed to be born again?"

Read aloud and summarize.

Questions. Don't argue about the meaning of "born of water and the Spirit." Instead, try to state in your own words what Jesus is getting at in 3:3-8. Since "born again" is a slogan these days, do your best to look at Jesus' words as though you have never heard them before.

Again, 3:16 is well known among Christians. Try to hear it in your hearts. Help the group to face up to the radical alternatives Jesus confronts you with in 3:16-21. Be as honest as possible about how you need to act on what He says.

Summarize and wrap up.

Worship. Praise God for the way His Spirit goes where He pleases. Thank Him for enabling you to be reborn. Thank the Father for His love in giving the Son to save you. Thank Him for enabling you to choose light rather than darkness.

1. Morris, page 216.
2. Morris, page 216.
3. E. Schweitzer, *"Pneuma," Theological Dictionary of the New Testament*, edited by Gerhard Kittel and Gerhard Friedrich, abridged in one volume by Geoffrey Bromiley (Grand Rapids, Michigan: William B. Eerdmans Publishing Company, 1985), pages 876-895.
4. Morris, pages 225-226.
5. Morris, page 227.
6. Morris, pages 871-873; Brown, volume 29, pages 497-499. For example, 5:20 and 16:27 use *phileo* for the Father's love for the Son, the Father's love for the disciples, and the disciples' love for the Father. In 3:35 and 14:23, John uses *agapao* for these loves. In 19:26, John is called "the disciple whom he loved" (*agapao*), but in 20:2 he is "the one Jesus loved" (*phileo*). Hebrew poetry is based on parallel synonyms, and John seems to be fond of using synonyms with no apparent change in meaning.
7. Donald Burdick, *The Letters of John the Apostle* (Chicago: Moody Press, 1985), page 284.
8. Morris, page 229.
9. Erich von Eicken and Helgo Lindner, "Apostle," *The New International Dictionary of New Testament Theology*, volume 1, page 128; see also Morris, page 230, footnote 78.

JOHN 4:1-54

Living Water

Jesus' miracles have made Him instantly popular in Judea. His success has attracted the attention of the Pharisees, who fancy themselves the watchdogs of genuine Judaism. But it is not yet time for Jesus to confront the Jewish leaders, so He abandons baptizing and returns to focus His ministry in Galilee. Yet Jesus is never off duty; a rest stop in Samaria has momentous results. Read 4:1-54.

Samaria (4:1-42)

He had to go through Samaria (4:4). Jesus had to go through Samaria not because of geography but because of His mission.

After King Solomon died in 931 BC, Israel split in two. The northern tribes called themselves Israel and made Samaria their capital city. The southern tribes were called Judah and kept Jerusalem as their capital. In 723 BC Assyria destroyed Israel, deported most of its population, and resettled the land with other conquered people. The whole region was now called Samaria. Most of the new mixed population began to practice a religion that combined elements of pagan religion with elements of biblical faith. The polytheism gradually faded, but Samaritan religion continued to be unique. The Samaritans regarded only the five books of Moses as Scripture; they rejected the Prophets

For Thought and Discussion: Do you think it is significant that this woman chose to draw water at noon rather than waiting until the more customary sunset? If so, how?

For Thought and Discussion: a. The title, "Savior of the world" (4:42) occurs only here and in 1 John 4:14. (Other parts of the New and Old Testaments call the Father "Savior.") What does this title imply about Jesus' identity and mission?
b. What does He save us from? For what purpose does He save us?

Optional Application: What difference does it make to you personally that Jesus is the Savior of the world?

and other books. They also sacrificed on Mount Gerizim instead of at Jerusalem.

The Jews (the people of Judah) regarded the Samaritans as in some ways worse than Gentiles because they worshiped the God of Israel in a corrupt fashion. In response, the Samaritans hated the Jews for rejecting them and also for taking over Galilee. Therefore, Samaritans often refused overnight shelter to Jews traveling between Galilee and Jerusalem for pilgrim feasts, and many Jews would rather go miles out of their way than set foot in Samaria.

Sixth hour (4:6). About noon. Sunset was the usual time *to draw water* (4:7), although noon was not unknown.[1]

Living water (4:10). This was the ordinary term for flowing water in a stream, as opposed to still water in a pond or well.

This mountain (4:20). Mount Gerizim. The rivalry between Jews and Samaritans centered on whether Jerusalem or Gerizim was the proper place for sacrifice. The Jews even destroyed the Samaritan temple on Gerizim in about 128 BC.[2]

I . . . am he (4:26). Literally, "I that speak to you, I am." This is the only time Jesus admitted that He was the Messiah before His trial. Among Jews the title had political associations that Jesus wanted to avoid, but to the Samaritans the Coming One was expected to be simply a prophet and a teacher.

Jesus uses this emphatic and unusual phrase "I am" many times in John's Gospel. It is the same one used in the Greek version of the Jewish Scriptures in Exodus 3:14; Deuteronomy 32:39; Isaiah 41:4, 43:10, 46:4, and other passages when God says "I AM" or "I am he."[3]

Talking with a woman (4:27). The rabbis avoided carrying on conversations with women of their own families, and to do so with any other woman was almost unheard of.[4]

1. How does Jesus apparently feel about Samaritans? (Give evidence from the story.)

_____

_____

_____

_____

_____

For Thought and Discussion: a. What evidence of Jesus' humanity do you find in 4:1-42?
  b. What signs of His deity do you find?

2. In what ways does Jesus' attitude toward women seem different from the usual Jewish attitude?

_____

_____

_____

Optional Application: Who are the "Samaritans" in your world—the people with whom decent or orthodox people have nothing to do? How can you treat one of them as Jesus treated the woman of Sychar? What would help such a person to recognize and believe in Jesus?

3. How does the woman of Sychar identify Jesus in each of the following verses?

4:9 _____

4:11 _____

4:19 _____

4:29 _____

For Thought and Discussion: a. What makes the woman think Jesus is a prophet?
  b. What convinces her that He is the Messiah?

4. How does Jesus draw the woman to discover who He is?

_____

_____

_____

_____

5. What does Jesus say about "living water" (4:10,13-14)?

_____

_____

_____

Optional Application: a. Is Jesus' living water leaping and welling up inside you? How is its presence or absence affecting your life?

b. What can you do to allow the living water to well up in you (4:14)?

Optional Application: When Jesus confronts you with sin and failure in your life, do you ever change the subject as the woman did (4:17-20)? Pray about this. When Jesus confronts you, why does He do it, and how does He want you to respond?

Optional Application: a. Do you worship God in spirit and truth? Think and pray about how you can do this more fully, with God's help. What kinds of things can block a person or group from worshiping in spirit and truth?

b. Pray for your church or fellowship to be able to worship in spirit and truth more. Ask God to help you set an example of true spiritual worship.

6. What do you think He means by "living water"? What does this vivid language evoke for you?

_____

_____

_____

_____

7. When Jesus reveals the woman's immoral life, she tries to change the subject back to "religion" and the dispute between Jews and Samaritans (4:19-20). However, how is Jesus' view of worship different from hers (4:21-24)?

Jesus	the woman

8. What do you think it means to worship "in spirit and in truth"?

_____

_____

_____

_____

_____

9. What did the disciples learn (about Jesus, themselves, their mission) from the encounter with the Samaritan woman (4:31-38)?

_____

_____

_____

_____

_____

_____

_____

10. Add 4:42 to your list about Jesus' identity on page 30.

Jesus heals the official's son (4:43-54)

Signs and wonders (4:48). "Wonders" suggests the purely miraculous and amazing. The people were interested in the spectacular, but not in signs that pointed to God and demanded a response of faith and allegiance.[5]

---

11. What moved each of the following people to believe in Jesus?

His disciples (1:35-49, 2:11) _____

_____

_____

the people in Jerusalem (2:23) _____

_____

the woman of Sychar (4:16-29) _____

_____

Optional Application: Meditate on 4:34. How true is this of you? How do you need to grow in this area? Ask God to show you His will and His work for you, and to empower you to do them. Make this a persistent prayer this week.

For Thought and Discussion: Why do you think Jesus went home to Galilee even when He knew 4:44 was true? What does this say about His character and His mission? (See 1:11.)

the other Samaritans of Sychar (4:39-42)

For Thought and Discussion:
a. Did Jesus accept people who believed because of His miracles (2:11, 6:26, 14:11, 20:30-31)? Why or why not?

b. Did faith based on miracles alone satisfy Jesus (2:23-24, 4:48, 20:29)? Why or why not?

c. What do you think mature faith is based on? (For an example, see James 1:2-5.)

d. What are the implications for your life?

For Thought and Discussion: How does 4:46-54 exemplify 20:29?

Optional Application: Are you in a position like the royal official's? If so, speak your desire to Jesus with the same persistence and faith, and trust His word of response (4:50). Ask God for this trust, and meditate on 4:50.

12. What is wrong with the kind of belief that is based only on seeing signs and wonders (4:48)?

13. How did Jesus require a deeper faith from the royal official (4:49-53)?

14. A sign points toward God, reveals the nature of Jesus' mission and character, and demands a response. How did this second sign at Cana do each of these things?

a. How did it point toward God?

b. What did it reveal about Jesus' mission and character?

_____

_____

c. What response did it demand?

_____

_____

_____

Your response

15. On page 30, write what you've learned about Jesus in chapter 4.

> **Study Skill—Application**
> When looking for ways to apply narrative portions of Scripture, try examining the characters to find examples to follow or avoid. For instance, you can look at the Samaritan woman's way of relating to Jesus, or Jesus' way of relating to her, or the values the woman shows in her conversation, or her actions after she encounters Jesus.

16. Review this lesson, looking for one principle, truth, or example that stands out to you for your own application. State this truth briefly.

_____

_____

_____

_____

_____

17. How do you need to grow in this area?

_____

_____

_____

18. What can you do to cooperate with God in making this happen?

_____

_____

_____

_____

_____

19. List any questions you have about chapter 4.

_____

_____

_____

For the group

Warm-up. Ask the group what water suggests to each person. What does it represent? What comes to mind when you think of running water?

Questions. Chapter 4 is packed with material for discussion. It's okay to spend your whole time on the woman at the well, or to take two meetings to cover the chapter. Don't go so fast that you overlook coming to terms with how each of you needs to act on what you've studied.

Worship. Thank Jesus for the spring of living water He puts into each person who comes to Him. Thank Him for His utter commitment to doing the will and the work of the One who sent Him, for being the Savior of the world.

1. Morris, page 258, cites Josephus, *Antiquities*, book 2, chapters 257-259.
2. Morris, pages 256, 268.
3. Morris, pages 273, 473.
4. Morris, page 274.
5. Morris, page 290.

JOHN 5:1-47

Opposition Begins

So far, the Evangelist has been showing how various people—the Baptist and his disciples, the villagers of Cana, the people of Jerusalem, a Pharisee, the Samaritans—have begun to learn about Jesus' identity and message. But as 2:12-25 made clear, Jesus' radical words and deeds were bound to win Him enemies. In 5:1–12:50 the Evangelist unfolds the increasingly bitter opposition Jesus attracted with His increasingly shocking ministry to the Jewish masses.

Running the vendors out of the Temple offended the priestly Sadducees. In 5:1-47, read what made the Pharisees, too, furious.

Study Skill—Helicopter or Microscope
When you look at a passage of Scripture, you can take in the big picture (the helicopter view) to see how it fits into the whole of the book, or you can take it apart (the microscope view) and look at the pieces. Both approaches are helpful and necessary to fully grasp the message the author intended to communicate. Practice using both views on chapter 5.

1. What major theme(s) stick out to you as you read 5:1-47?

_____

_____

For Thought and Discussion: a. Put yourself in the invalid's position. What reasons might he have had for remaining by the pool for all those years? What does his situation reveal about his character and personality?
   b. How would you have felt if you were the invalid and were asked whether you wanted to get well?

For Thought and Discussion: Why would a sick person not want to become whole? What are some advantages of having a physical illness or a spiritual or emotional wound?

_____

_____

_____

_____

_____

2. What is the relationship between this chapter and the previous section?

_____

_____

_____

_____

3. Describe any major shift in focus you see from chapter 4 to chapter 5.

_____

_____

_____

_____

Now take a microscope view.

Equal with God (5:1-30)

4. Why do you think Jesus asked the invalid if he wanted to get well (5:6)?

_____

_____

_____

_____

5. The invalid doesn't answer Jesus' question. What does his reply in 5:7 tell you about him and his focus?

_____

_____

_____

_____

_____

6. Does this man's healing depend on his faith (5:6-8)? How can you tell, and why is this important?

_____

_____

_____

_____

_____

_____

_____

Optional Application: a. Can you think of any areas of your own life where you are like this invalid?
   b. Ask yourself Jesus' question in 5:6. Then ask yourself (and God) what you should do about your answer.

For Thought and Discussion: a. What might be the "something worse" that will happen to the healed man if he doesn't stop sinning?
   b. In the Gospels, Jesus doesn't normally say this to people He heals. Why do you suppose He warns this man?

For Thought and Discussion: The Jewish leaders utterly ignore the fact that a man has been miraculously healed (5:10-12,16). Why? What does this say about them? Are you like them in any way?

The law forbids (5:10). The Law of Moses forbids work on the Sabbath. The rabbis minutely spelled out what constituted work (by 200 AD thirty-nine classes of work were defined). Nehemiah 13:15 and Jeremiah 17:21-27 condemn carrying loads for commercial business on the Sabbath, so the rabbis decided that "taking out aught from one domain into another"[1] was always work. This included carrying a mat. The rabbis had a theory that each commandment should be applied as widely as possible to avoid even accidentally breaking the law.

---

7. Jesus speaks about Himself in 5:17-47. As you examine His words, consider what they teach about Him, and take the opportunity to praise and worship Jesus as you study.

For Thought and Discussion: In 5:19, Jesus says, "the Son . . . can do only what he sees his Father doing." How is 2:1-11 an example of Jesus doing what He sees the Father doing?

For Thought and Discussion: a. In 5:25 Jesus speaks of a time that "has now come." Who are the dead who already hear and live?
   b. In 5:28-29 He speaks of a time that is still future. How will that resurrection be different from the one in 5:25?
   c. Why is Jesus qualified to judge all people (5:27,30)?

For Further Study: a. On what basis will Jesus judge us all (Matthew 25:31-46, John 5:29, Romans 2:6-11, 2 Corinthians 5:10)?
   b. Does this contradict the idea that we are saved from condemnation simply by putting our faith in Jesus? Why or why not?
   c. What light does John 6:27-29 shed on this topic?

8. What reasons emerge from chapter 5 for the Jewish leaders' opposition to Jesus?

5:16 _____

_____

5:18 _____

_____

5:43 _____

_____

9. In what areas does Jesus claim to be equal with God the Father?

5:17 _____

_____

5:19 _____

_____

5:20 _____

_____

5:21 _____

_____

5:22-23 _____

_____

5:24 _____

_____

5:26 _____

_____

10. On page 30, jot a summary of your answers in question 9.

___

The Father raises the dead (5:21). The Sadducees rejected the idea of resurrection. But the Pharisees, along with most ordinary Jews, believed firmly that the Father could raise the dead at any time (Deuteronomy 32:39, 1 Samuel 2:6, 2 Kings 5:7) and would raise the dead on the last day. However, the Jews were equally clear that no one but God could raise the dead.[2]

Testimony (5:31-47)

Testimony is important to the Evangelist. He has already recorded the witness of several people to Jesus, and now he gives us Jesus' words on the subject.

My testimony is not valid (5:31). If Jesus' words are the only evidence that He is intimately related to the Father, then His claim must be false.

Study Skill—Lists
Be alert for lists of commands, promises, reasons, etc. in a passage. Question 11 points you to a subtle list in 5:33-46.

---

11. What witnesses to His identity does Jesus name?

5:33-35 _____

5:36 _____

5:37 _____

5:39 _____

5:46 _____

Work (5:36). Jesus speaks often of "work" and "works." He is usually referring to the Father's work(s) that He, Jesus, is doing. These works include the miraculous "signs" of transforming things, healing, and raising the dead. But they also include Jesus' teaching and all His other

Optional Application: Consider Jesus' example in 5:30. What does this mean for you? Ask God to show you how you can follow Jesus' example. Meditate and pray about this verse daily this week.

For Thought and Discussion: What witnesses testify about Jesus besides those named in 5:33-46? See 15:26-27.

For Thought and Discussion: With Jesus standing before them, how could the Jewish leaders have failed to see or hear God (5:37-38)?

71

For Further Study:
Do a word study on
work and *works* in
John's Gospel. What
do you learn about
Jesus' mission and
the mission He gave
His disciples?

**Optional
Application:** Are you
at all like the Phari-
sees in 5:39-44? If
so, what can you do
about this?

actions day to day as the manifestation of God.
Indeed, His very presence in the world is His
mission, His work.

Whereas John usually calls Jesus' miracles
"signs," Jesus calls them and everything else He
does "work(s)." Unlike "sign" and "miracle,"
"work" is a mundane word. It implies that both
Jesus' natural and His supernatural actions are
simply His work, His job, just as other men
have their jobs. But Jesus' work comes from the
Father and points to the Father; in the Old Testament, God's "works" are involved with creat-
ing and delivering His people from slavery
(Genesis 2:2-3; Psalm 8:3, 66:5-7).[3]

---

12. For what faults does Jesus rebuke the Pharisees
in 5:39-44? Record as many as you can find.

_____

_____

_____

_____

_____

_____

Moses . . . wrote about me (5:46). "Moses wrote of
Christ, as the seed of the woman that shall
bruise the serpent's head [Genesis 3:15], as the
seed of Abraham by which all the nations of the
earth shall be blessed [Genesis 12:3], as the
Shiloh unto whom shall be the gathering of the
people [Genesis 49:10], as the Star out of Jacob,
and Sceptre that shall rise out of Israel
[Numbers 24:17], as the Great Prophet whom
God will raise up and unto whom the Jews
should hearken [Deuteronomy 18:15]. Moreover, the moral law of Moses, by revealing the
holy will of God and setting up a standard of
human righteousness in conformity with that
will, awakens a knowledge of sin and guilt
[Romans 3:20, 7:7], and thus serves as a school-

master to bring us to Christ [Galatians 3:24]. Finally, the ritual law and all the ceremonies of Mosaic worship were [types] of the Christian dispensation [Colossians 2:17], as the healing serpent in the wilderness pointed to Christ on the cross [Numbers 21:9, John 3:14]."[4]

Your response

13. Summarize the points Jesus makes in John 5:1-47.

_____

_____

_____

_____

_____

_____

14. What one truth from this lesson seems most significant to you today?

_____

_____

_____

_____

15. What implications does this truth have for your life?

_____

_____

_____

_____

16. What can you do this week to act on these implications more, by God's grace?

_____

_____

_____

_____

17. List any questions you have about chapter 5.

_____

_____

_____

For the group

Warm-up. Ask, "What would you think and say if Jesus asked you, 'Do you want to get well?'"

Questions. Unless you plan to take two meetings for your discussion, you should choose one or two aspects of chapter 5 to focus on. This will prevent you from having a shallow discussion that fails to grapple with the astounding implications of what Jesus says and does. Try to put yourselves in the shoes of the paralytic when he is talking with Jesus, and consider how you are in a similar position. Or, put yourselves in the place of the Jewish leaders as Jesus claims equality to God in work, having life, giving life, judgment, or honor. What difference does it make to your lives, priorities, attitudes, and actions that each of these facts is true of Jesus? How will you act differently this week because of these things?

Worship. Praise Jesus and the Father for what chapter 5 reveals about Them: Their desire and ability to heal, Their constant work, Their gift of life to you, Their worthiness to judge all people, the many witnesses They have given about Themselves.

1. Morris, page 306, note 28.
2. Morris, page 314; *The NIV Study Bible*, edited by Kenneth Barker (Grand Rapids, Michigan: Zondervan Corporation, 1985), page 1476.
3. Morris, pages 688-691.
4. John Peter Lange, *Lange's Commentary on the Holy Scriptures: Volume 17: John* (Grand Rapids, Michigan: Zondervan Corporation, n.d.), pages 197-198.

JOHN 6:1-71

The Bread of Life

John has recorded several signs that contrast the new way of Jesus with the old way of Judaism. Jesus' new wine, made from the water of ritual purification, is far better than the old wine (2:10). Jesus' body is the new Temple that will make the old one obsolete (2:19-21). The old way of law-keeping will not help a Pharisee enter the Kingdom; he must be born anew (3:3). The old ways of worshiping are being replaced by worship "in spirit and truth" (4:23).

A second theme John has introduced is how Jesus gives life. Living water replaces the dead water the Samaritan woman was drinking (4:13-14); the royal official's son is saved from near death (4:50); the paralytic receives a healthy life (5:8)—the Son is the source of life (1:4; 5:21,24-26).

Both of these themes—newness and life—appear in chapter 6. Ask God to reveal the truth about Himself to you as you read 6:1-71.

Five thousand fed (6:1-15)

Because they saw the miraculous signs (6:2). John omits most of this ministry in Galilee on which the Synoptics focus. It is now almost another *Passover* (6:4), so either six months or a full year have passed since the events of chapter 5.

Gave thanks (6:11). Jews customarily blessed God (not the food) before they ate, saying something

75

like, "Blessed are You, O Lord God of the universe, who has given us bread from the earth."

The Prophet (6:41). Moses fed the Israelites with manna (Exodus 16). Elisha also miraculously fed a hundred men (2 Kings 4:42-44). Therefore, the Jews concluded that Jesus must be the Prophet like Moses foretold in Deuteronomy 18:15.

1. How does this fourth miracle recorded by John function as a sign?

   a. How does it point toward God (and to what aspect of God's nature does it point)?

   _____

   _____

   _____

   _____

   b. What does it reveal about Jesus' mission and character?

   _____

   _____

   _____

   _____

   c. What response does it invite?

   _____

   _____

   _____

   _____

2. For the first time, Jesus had His disciples participate in this miracle. Why do you think He did this?

   _____

_____

_____

_____

Walking on water (6:16-21)

According to Mark, Jesus sent His disciples away ahead of Him (Mark 6:45-46). He probably wanted "to deal with the would-be king-makers without the presence of His own close followers."[1] Once again John records how people misunderstood who Jesus was and what the Messiah was supposed to be and do (John 6:14-15).

The sign in 6:16-21 is for the disciples alone. At the Passover meal, later Jews recalled how God made a way through the Red Sea when man could not (Psalm 77:19, 78:13) before He fed His people with manna (Psalm 78:24).[2]

3. What does Jesus reveal about Himself in John 6:16-21?

_____

_____

_____

_____

Bread from heaven (6:22-59)

4. As in 3:3, Jesus ignores what the people say (6:25) and instead speaks to the thoughts in their hearts. What is wrong with the reason the people are seeking Jesus (6:26-27)?

_____

_____

_____

For Further Study: Compare Psalm 107:4-9,23-32 to what happens in John 6.

Optional Application: How is Jesus' ability in 6:16-21 relevant to you personally? Do you really believe He will do this in your life? Pray about this.

For Thought and Discussion: a. What do you learn about the people from the way they emphasize "do" and "works" in 6:28?

b. Are you like this in any way? Ask God to show you.

77

For Further Study:
A topical Bible or commentary might lead you from John 6:27 to Isaiah 55:1-2. What is the connection between these two passages?

For Thought and Discussion: What is the relationship between work and faith in John 6:27-29? Compare this passage to Ephesians 2:4-10 and James 2:14-26.

Seal (6:27). Since many people were illiterate in those days, a seal was often stamped in wax on an object to show who owned it. Also, a seal authenticated a document as bearing a particular person's authority and approval. An object such as a sacrificial animal could be sealed to show that it was set apart for a particular purpose (10:36).[3]

What must we do (6:28). The Jews missed what Jesus said in 6:27 about *giving* them the food that endures to eternal life. The rabbis sometimes spoke of the Law as the heavenly food that God gives and by which a person can attain life.[4]

The work of God (6:29). This is another of John's double meanings: it can be the work that God desires people to do, or the work that God accomplishes in people.[5]

5. a. In what sense is faith in Jesus a human "work" (6:29)?

b. In what sense is it different from a work done to earn God's favor?

What will you do (6:30). If Jesus had given the
people a list of commands by which to please
God, they might have been content. But He
says, "Believe in Me." For that they want a sign
greater than the one that confirmed Moses' ministry. So far, Jesus has only fed five thousand
men once, but Moses (actually, God) fed the
whole nation for forty years.

6. The people want Jesus to reenact the miracle of
the bread from heaven. Write down everything
Jesus says about the bread from heaven in
6:32-35,48-59.

_____

_____

_____

_____

_____

_____

_____

_____

**For Thought and
Discussion:** What is
implied by the phrase
"the bread of life"?

**For Thought and
Discussion:** John
contrasted Jesus with
the bread the Jews
mistakenly sought—
manna and the Law.
What kinds of "bread"
do modern people
mistakenly seek to
satisfy their hungers?

True bread (6:32). "True" is a frequent and important word in John's Gospel. The manna was a
foreshadow; Jesus is the real bread, the reality
to which the manna pointed. Also, bread symbolized the Law in Jewish writings, but Jesus is
the bread that fully satisfies, as the Law cannot.
    In the same way, Jesus is the "true light"
(1:9), the real light that was only foreshadowed
by the light of the Law. He is also the "true
vine" (15:1).

7. Belief in Jesus is essential (6:35,47). How is it
possible for a person to believe (6:36-40,43-46)?

79

For Thought and Discussion: a. Why is it good news that our constant faith does not ultimately depend on our efforts (6:37-39)?

b. Does this relieve us of responsibility for believing in and obeying Jesus? Why or why not?

c. How can faith depend on God and on us at the same time?

Optional Application: Are you still looking for sustenance in anything less than the true bread? Or, have you eaten and drunk Jesus once for all, and do you eat and drink Jesus regularly? How is this affecting your life?

_____

_____

_____

_____

_____

My flesh, which I will give (6:51). On the Cross.

Eat the flesh . . . drink his blood (6:53). Eating flesh was a crude, graphic, attention-getting way of expressing Jesus' thought. Drinking blood was probably even more disgusting to Jews than eating human flesh, for Leviticus 17:10-12 explicitly forbids drinking blood.

Remains (6:56). This word, which is translated "endures" in 6:27, is another key word for John. KJV and NASB often render it as "to abide." It is especially frequent in 15:1-10. It suggests a constant, permanent relationship of being together with.

8. What do you think Jesus means by saying that we must eat His flesh and drink His blood (6:53)?

_____

_____

_____

Responses (6:60-71)

Disciples (6:60). Jesus had many followers besides the Twelve, whom He called apostles. The miracles had inspired many to a certain degree of belief and desire to follow this rabbi.

Hard (6:60). The Greek word implies "harsh," that is, hard to accept, not hard to understand.[6]

9. Why did many of Jesus' disciples cease to follow Him after hearing the discourse in 6:25-59? (See 6:41-42,52-66.)

_____

_____

_____

_____

_____

10. Why didn't the Twelve abandon Jesus (6:67-69)?

_____

_____

_____

_____

_____

For Thought and Discussion: Is having to eat and drink Jesus still a stumbling block for modern would-be disciples? Explain.

For Thought and Discussion: What does 6:63 have to do with the discussion at hand?

For Thought and Discussion: a. What does 6:64-65,70-71 tell you about Jesus?
b. Why do you think John considered this important to tell at this point?

Your response

11. Summarize what 6:1-71 adds to John's story of Jesus. (Add your thoughts to page 30.)

12. What truth from this chapter would you like to actively apply to your own life this week?

_____

_____

_____

_____

13. How is it relevant to you?

_____

_____

81

_____

_____

_____

14. What action can you take to put this truth into practice?

_____

_____

_____

_____

15. List any questions you have about 6:1-71.

_____

_____

_____

For the group

Warm-up. Ask, "What does bread symbolize for you?"

Questions. Your chief task here is to interpret the symbolic actions (6:1-21) and words (6:22-59) that Jesus does and says. Focus on the meaning of the true bread. Then get personal: How does each of you need to respond actively to what Jesus has done and said?

Worship. Praise Jesus for being the true and living bread from heaven. Praise Him for being the sole source of life for you, your only hope of survival. Thank Him for showing you how to abandon all alternate sources of survival.

1. Morris, page 348.
2. Brown, volume 29, page 255.
3. Morris, page 359; Brown, volume 29, page 261.
4. Morris, page 360.
5. Brown, volume 29, page 262.
6. Morris, page 382.

LESSON NINE

JOHN 7:1-52

Who Is Jesus?

The prominent Jews of Judea are still furious at
Jesus for what He said and did in Jerusalem over a
year ago: He not only worked on the Sabbath, but
He even claimed the right to do so because He was
equal with God (5:18)! For this, the Jewish leaders
want Him dead.

But Jesus has not appeared in Judea since that
confrontation. Instead, He has worked His miracles
and proclaimed His shocking teaching in Galilee.
He has made a name for Himself in those parts, but
He and His brothers both know that what happens
in Galilee is not what counts. Someone who claims
to be the Messiah must prove His claim before the
whole nation, and that means in the capital city,
not in some provincial villages.

Six months have passed since the miraculous
feeding. Jesus has spent long enough in Galilee—
His hour is coming. But the hour has not yet come.
The Father has appointed the moment of Jesus' death,
and Jesus weighs every action to fit that timing.

Read 7:1-52, keeping in mind these questions—
they should be part of any overview of a passage:

1. What place does this chapter have in the
   fulfillment of Jesus' mission?
2. What place does this chapter have in John's
   purpose for writing this book?

Tabernacles (7:2). This feast was so important to
the Jews that they often referred to it (not Pass-

For Thought and Discussion: a. What attitudes about ministry and messiahship do Jesus' brothers show in 7:3-5? b. Do you ever have similar feelings about your own or another's ministry? What is good or bad about those attitudes?

For Thought and Discussion: How do Jesus' words in chapter 7 reflect the themes of Tabernacles? What point was He making?

over) as *the* Feast.[1] It was held when the year's harvest was gathered in, so it celebrated first of all the people's thanks for a good harvest (Exodus 23:16). Second, it commemorated God's care for Israel during the desert wandering (Leviticus 23:33-43, Deuteronomy 16:13-15). For this reason, the pilgrims lived for the week in tents (huts, booths, tabernacles) made of branches.

"The feast was also associated with the triumphant 'day of the Lord.'"[2] On that day the Lord would use the nations to punish Jerusalem, then would punish the nations, and finally would become "king over the whole earth" (Zechariah 14:9). "Living water" (14:8) would flow from Jerusalem to the world. And every year, all the nations would come to Jerusalem to celebrate Tabernacles, or they would have no rain (14:16-19). Thus, Tabernacles was linked not only with living water, rain, and the harvest, but also with the ingathering of the nations at the end of the age.

If rain fell during Tabernacles, it was considered a sign that the autumn rains would be abundant. The prayer for rain was dramatized each morning, when a procession descended the temple hill to a fountain. "There a priest filled a golden pitcher with water, as the choir repeated [Isaiah 12:3]: 'With joy you will draw water from the wells of salvation.' Then the procession went up to the Temple through the Water Gate." The crowd carried bundles of branches, called *lulabs*, and citrus fruits (Leviticus 23:40) as symbols of the leafy huts and the harvest. They sang praise psalms and danced. "When they reached the altar of holocausts in front of the Temple, they proceeded around the altar waving the *lulabs* and singing [Psalm 118:25]. Then the priest went up the ramp to the altar to pour the water into a silver funnel whence it flowed into the ground."[3] Later Jewish writings connect Isaiah 12:3 in this ceremony with the outpouring of the Holy Spirit.[4]

The Jews . . . the crowds (7:11-13). The former are the leaders who are Jesus' enemies. The latter are the "uninformed majority"[5] (who are also Jews), many of whom are probably pilgrims from outside Jerusalem. They know nothing about the plot of the authorities (7:20) and little about Jesus' teaching. A third group, *the people of Jerusalem* (7:25), are not among the plotters, but they know about the scheme.

1. What speculations and opinions are circulating among the various groups in Jerusalem before Jesus arrives for the Feast (7:1,12)?

_____

_____

_____

_____

Without having studied (7:15). The KJV reads, "How knoweth this man letters, having never learned?" The sentence does not imply that Jesus was illiterate (few Jewish men were). It means that Jesus was apparently able to quote large amounts of Scripture and discuss it at length like the rabbis, but He had never studied under a rabbi. This was unheard of.[6]

Not my own (7:16). "Had He said that He was self-taught, or that He needed no teacher, or the like, He would have been discredited immediately. The age did not prize originality. The Rabbinic method was to cite authorities for all important statements. So Jesus does not claim to be the originator of His message."[7]

2. a. Despite their hostility, the Jewish leaders are impressed by Jesus' knowledge of Scripture. According to Jesus, from where did He get His teaching (7:16)?

_____

b. How could His hearers verify this (7:17)?

_____

_____

85

For Thought and Discussion: How does a person choose to do God's will (7:17)? What does this involve in your life?

c. Why do you think this is the only way to know if Jesus' words are true?

_____

_____

_____

_____

_____

The law (7:19). The Jewish leaders were breaking it by plotting against an innocent man, among other ways.

Circumcision (7:22). The Jews considered the command to circumcise on the eighth day (Leviticus 12:3) to be so binding that it even took precedence over the Sabbath. The ceremonial and thus the spiritual needs of a man (to assure that he was part of the covenant community) took priority. Jesus was not saying that the Sabbath should not be kept, but that even the Jews recognized that some acts not only may be done but must be done on the Sabbath because of what the Sabbath meant.[8]

3. Why did Jesus think that healing was perfectly appropriate on the Sabbath (7:21-24)?

_____

_____

_____

_____

_____

4. How did the Jews' opposition to healing on the Sabbath prove that they were "judging by mere appearances" (7:24)?

_____

_____

_____

_____

_____

_____

5. The Jews were judging Jesus' identity based on
   where He was born and raised (7:25-27,40-43).
   Was this judging by mere appearances? If so,
   how should the Jews have gone about deciding
   who Jesus was?

_____

_____

_____

_____

_____

6. a. Describe a situation in which you are cur-
      rently tempted to judge by appearances.

_____

_____

_____

_____

_____

b. On what basis should you judge this situation instead?

_____

_____

_____

_____

_____

For Thought and Discussion: What was wrong with the people's reason in 7:27 for rejecting Jesus (7:28-29)?

For Thought and Discussion: Why is 7:30 important? (Compare 10:17-18.)

Study Skill—Context
Verse 24 is a key to understanding the debate in chapter 7. The focus of the chapter, as well as of the book, is "Who is Jesus?" Notice how reading individual verses in the context of the whole chapter and book can help you follow what is going on.

No one will know (7:27). There was disagreement and uncertainty about the Messiah's origins. Because of Micah 5:2, some thought He would come from Bethlehem (Matthew 2:4-6, John 7:42). Others believed that the Messiah would remain hidden until He suddenly appeared to His people.[9]

Pharisees (7:32). They "would have their finger on the public pulse more than the chief priests who were more remote." Also, in their role as the nation's spiritual watchdogs, the Pharisees were more interested in and actively opposed to Jesus' words and deeds. "But the chief priests were in the place of power. More effective action was possible by combining with them."[10]

7. In 7:33-34, Jesus changes the topic from where He is from to where He is going. What do you think He means?

_____

_____

_____

_____

_____

Scattered among the Greeks (7:35). "The Dispersion" (NASB; Greek: *diaspora*) was "a technical term for the large number of Jews who at this time were dispersed throughout the Roman

Empire and beyond."[11] Jews had been spreading through the known world since the Babylonians exiled them from Palestine six hundred years earlier. Ironically, Jesus' disciples later launched their international ministry among precisely this group (see the book of Acts).

Cried out . . . said in a loud voice (7:28,37). The Gospels rarely record Jesus raising His voice. A rabbi normally sat to teach, but in 7:37 Jesus *stood* to proclaim His message like a prophet.[12]

For Further Study: The Jews were speculating that Jesus might be planning to go and teach the Greeks—Gentiles (7:35). How does this compare with what happens in the book of Acts?

For Further Study: Compare John 7:37-39 to Isaiah 55:1-2.

Study Skill—Personalizing the Verbs
To help yourself see how a passage is personally relevant, read it with an eye to the verbs. Ask yourself, "What does it mean for me to do that?" or "How can I tell when I'm doing that?" Questions 8 and 9 personalize 7:37-39 in this way.

---

8. Read what Jesus promises to those who come to Him (7:37-39). What does it mean for *you* to come to Jesus and drink (7:37)?

_____

_____

_____

_____

_____

9. How can you tell when streams of living water are flowing from within you?

_____

_____

_____

_____

_____

For Thought and Discussion: Why did Jesus have to die before the Spirit could come to us? (Consider: What did Jesus' death accomplish, and what is the Spirit's work?)

For Thought and Discussion: Why do you think 7:21-24, 28-29,33-34,37-38 made some people suspect that Jesus was the Prophet or the Christ?

For Further Study: Make a list of all the misunderstandings of Jesus in chapter 7 or in chapters 1-7. Be sure you know the truth about each thing that people misunderstood.

For Thought and Discussion: What is ironic about 7:50-51 in light of 7:19 and 7:48-49?

Glorified (7:39). The Crucifixion was the moment when Jesus was glorified—His greatest shame was His greatest glory. Jesus had to die before the Holy Spirit could be given to men and women.

10. What was wrong with the reason in 7:41-42 for rejecting Jesus? (*Optional:* See Luke 2:1-6.)

_____

_____

_____

_____

A prophet does not come out of Galilee (7:52). The Pharisees "were angry—and wrong. Jonah came from Galilee, and perhaps other prophets as well. Moreover, the Pharisees overlooked the right of God to raise up prophets from wherever He chooses."[13] Judeans, especially the prominent men, despised Galileans as unsophisticated and lax in religious practice.[14]

11. On page 30, write down what chapter 7 reveals about Jesus' identity and mission.

12. Summarize what 7:1-52 is about.

what Jesus says and does _____

_____

_____

_____

_____

how various people respond _____

_____

90

_____

_____

_____

_____

_____

For Further Study:
Examine each question asked in chapter 7. How would you answer each? What do the questions show about the askers?

Your response

13. What is the most personally significant truth you found in chapter 7?

_____

_____

_____

_____

_____

14. How would you like this truth to affect your life? How do you need to grow in this area?

_____

_____

_____

_____

_____

15. What can you do this week to let this effect take place in your life increasingly?

_____

_____

_____

_____

_____

16. List any questions you have about 7:1-52.

_____

_____

_____

_____

For the group

Warm-up. Ask each person to name one reason for rejecting Jesus that he or she has heard. When you finish discussing 7:1-52, you can compare the reasons you named to the ones the Jews thought of. How are they similar and different?

Questions. As you study chapter 7 through the microscope, keep coming back to the helicopter view in question 12. Emphasize 7:24 and 7:37-39.

Worship. Praise God for fulfilling the Feast of Tabernacles by sending the Holy Spirit as the true living water that brings an abundant harvest. Thank Him for satisfying your thirst. Praise Jesus for never losing sight of His heavenly origin, the nature and timing of His mission, and His heavenly goal.

1. Morris, page 394.
2. Brown, volume 29, page 326.
3. Brown, volume 29, page 327.
4. Morris, pages 420-421.
5. Morris, page 402.
6. Morris, pages 404-405.
7. Morris, page 405.
8. Morris, pages 408-409.
9. Brown, volume 29, page 53.
10. Morris, page 415.
11. Morris, page 418.
12. Morris, page 422.
13. *The NIV Study Bible*, page 1611.
14. Morris, page 434, note 108.

LESSON TEN

JOHN 8:12-9:41

The Light of the World

The Feast of Tabernacles has just ended. Most of the
crowds are leaving, but Jesus remains, for He has
more to do and proclaim on this visit. Fearlessly He
reveals Himself so that those with eyes may be
saved, and those with none may be without excuse.

Chapters 8 and 9 have related themes, so we
will cover them together in two lessons. Read them
through, observing how the tension between Jesus
and His opponents is intensifying.

1. In a way 8:12-59 and 9:1-41 are separate episodes, and in a way they are connected.

   a. What would you say is the main point being
   made in each episode?

   8:12-59 _____

   _____

   _____

   _____

   9:1-41 _____

   _____

   _____

   _____

   _____

b. What themes tie the two episodes together?

_____

_____

_____

_____

_____

_____

_____

I am (8:12,24,28,58; 9:5). See the note on 4:26
(page 60).

The light (8:12, 9:5). Jesus is alluding to another
theme of Tabernacles. Just before Zechariah
prophesied the living water flowing out from
Jerusalem, he predicted that the day of the Lord
would be unique because there would be light
in the evening (Zechariah 14:6-7). Isaiah
60:19-20 explained that the Lord Himself would
replace the sun and moon as the light in that
day (compare Revelation 21:23-25, 22:5). Just as
God provided water from a rock in the desert for
Israel, and that rock typified Christ (Exodus
17:1-7, 1 Corinthians 10:4), so God guided the
desert wanderers in the night with a pillar of
flame (Exodus 13:21). Water and light were
linked symbols.

   On the first night of Tabernacles (and perhaps on the others) "there was a ritual of light-
ing four golden candlesticks in the Court of the
Women. Each of these . . . had four golden
bowls on top which were reached by ladders.
Floating in these bowls were wicks made from
the drawers and girdles of the priests; and when
they were lit, it is said that all Jerusalem
reflected the light that burned in the House of
Water Drawing (that part of the Court of the
Women through which the water procession
passed—see above, page [84])."[1]

   Also, light symbolized both the Law and
God Himself (Psalms 36:9, 119:105).

2. Write down what Jesus claims about Himself
and His words in 8:12-9:41.

8:12, 9:5 _____

_____

_____

8:19 _____

_____

8:23 _____

_____

8:29 _____

_____

_____

8:31-32 _____

_____

_____

8:51 _____

_____

8:56,58 _____

_____

_____

9:39 _____

_____

_____

**For Thought and
Discussion:** Explain
each of Jesus' claims
in question 2.

Appearing as your own witness (8:13). The Pharisees have nothing to say about the truth or
falsehood of Jesus' radical claim. "Typically,
they fasten on a legal technicality."[2] According
to their interpretation of the Law, one who tes-

For Further Study:
Compare your answer
for question 3 to
5:13-47.

tifies about himself can be ignored. They failed
to see that light quite validly testifies to being
light simply by shining.

3. What evidence verifies that Jesus' claims are
valid (8:14-18,28)?

_____

_____

_____

_____

The place where the offerings were put (8:20). A
section of the Court of the Women. In other
words, Jesus spoke these words near where the
candles that had burned during Tabernacles
were now extinguished.

The blind will see (9:39). "Giving sight to the blind
was predicted as a Messianic activity"[3] (Isaiah
29:18, 35:5, 42:7), and Jesus did this kind of
miracle more often than any other.

4. What do you think Jesus means when He calls
Himself "the light of the world" (8:12;
9:4-5,39)?

_____

_____

_____

_____

_____

_____

5. How does the sign in 9:1-7 demonstrate this
aspect of His mission and identity?

_____

_____

_____

_____

_____

For Thought and Discussion: What does the former blind man testify about Jesus? What does this reveal about Jesus' identity and mission?

6. In each of the following verses, what does the former blind man call Jesus, and how does he treat Him?

   9:11 _____

   9:17 _____

   9:33 _____

   9:35-38 _____

   _____

   _____

Optional Application: How is the former blind man's testimony before hostile inquisitors a model for you (9:10-11,15,17,25, 30-33)?

7. How do these comments further illustrate the way in which Jesus is the light of the world?

   _____

   _____

   _____

   _____

   _____

8. At the same time, Jesus says that in the presence of His light "those who see will become blind" (9:39). How do the Pharisees in chapter 9 illustrate this?

   _____

   _____

   _____

   _____

   _____

For Thought and Discussion: Why couldn't the Pharisees see that Jesus was the light?

Optional Application: Are you ever like the Pharisees, putting preconceived theology ahead of clear evidence of Jesus' deeds and desires? Pray about this.

Have never been slaves (8:33). These Jews were forgetting the Romans whose rule so chafed Jewish pride.

A Samaritan and demon-possessed (8:48). First, they were accusing Jesus of keeping the Law as falsely as the Samaritans and of having the Samaritans' disrespect for the Jews' exclusive heritage. Second, they were charging Jesus with being demonic, which Jesus considered extremely heinous (Matthew 12:24-32).[4]

9. How do Jesus' opponents in chapter 8 display their blindness?

8:12-15 _____

_____

_____

8:22,25,27 _____

_____

_____

8:33,39,41 _____

_____

_____

8:53 _____

_____

_____

Your response

10. What one insight from this lesson stands out to you as something you want to take to heart?

_____

_____

_____

_____

_____

11. How is this relevant to you? How do you fall
short or need to grow in this area?

_____

_____

_____

_____

12. What can you do about this during the coming
week?

_____

_____

_____

_____

13. List any questions you have about this lesson.

_____

_____

_____

_____

For the group

Because the themes of light and sight run through
8:12-9:41, lesson ten lets you examine all the material on those themes. Lesson eleven will cover the
other major themes of 7:53-9:41—sin and
judgment.

Warm-up. Ask what light represents or symbolizes
for each person in the group.

Questions. Light, sight, and blindness are the themes in this lesson. Focus on what Jesus means by calling Himself the light of the world, and on how 8:12-9:41 illustrates both this truth and the way Jesus describes His mission in 9:39. Then evaluate your own lives in light of 9:39. Are you more like the healed man or like the Pharisees with regard to sight and blindness? What practical difference does it make to each of your lives that Jesus is the light of the world?

If you have time, discuss the meaning and implications of Jesus' claims in question 2. Lesson eleven is short, so you may be able to come back to this question in your next meeting.

Worship. Praise Jesus for being the light of the world, for coming so that those who want light and sight will have them, and for blinding those who don't want to see reality and truth. Ask Him to give you each a deep desire to see what is real, rather than the illusions and false preconceptions that surround you.

1. Brown, volume 29, page 344.
2. Morris, page 439.
3. *The NIV Study Bible*, page 1614.
4. Morris, pages 466-467.

JOHN 7:53-9:41

Sin and Judgment

Jesus came into the world not to condemn it, but to save it (3:17). Yet, the Father "has entrusted all judgment to the Son" (5:22), and Jesus says, "For judgment I have come into this world" (9:39). In a sense, men and women judge themselves by their reactions to Jesus—by whether they choose light, belief, and sight, or darkness, unbelief, and blindness (3:18-21, 9:39).

Sin and judgment were major issues for the law-minded Jews, and they are major issues for Jesus and His Father. Read 7:53-9:41 again, this time noticing how John weaves Jesus' teaching on sin and judgment into the debates about light and sight.

The adulteress (7:53-8:11)[1]

Mount of Olives (8:1). During His final stay in Jerusalem, Jesus spent His nights on this mountain a mile or two from the city (Luke 21:37). He had friends in Bethany, a village on the mount (John 11:1), and He was fond of a certain olive grove on the mount (Luke 22:39, John 18:1).

Caught in adultery (8:3). There almost certainly must have been a trap set for the woman. Jewish law required that two witnesses actually see the physical act in order to convict someone of

101

For Thought and Discussion: a. In 8:7, is Jesus saying that no judge has the right to pass sentence unless he is sinless? Why or why not? What are the implications of this view for a legal system, a family, or a church?

b. Is Jesus speaking in 8:7 strictly to lynch mobs, accusers with base motives, people indulging private vindictiveness, and others who take the law into their own hands? What are the implications of this view?

c. Does 8:7 suggest that Jesus opposes punishing adultery or opposes the death penalty? Why or why not?

For Thought and Discussion: What was Jesus' goal for the woman, rather than punishing her as she deserved? How is this an example for us?

adultery. But the equally guilty man was not arrested—someone let him escape. Also, the woman's husband was curiously absent from this scene. Further, Jewish procedure dictated that a person must be warned once and given a chance to repent before action was taken, but there is no hint of a warning. Finally, there was no need, other than vindictiveness against the woman, that she be brought into the temple courts for a public accusation.[2]

The scene was also a *trap* (8:6) for Jesus. The Law of Moses commanded that the Jews stone not only *such women* (8:5)—the accusers deliberately used the feminine form—but also the men involved (Leviticus 20:10, Deuteronomy 22:22). The legal experts ignored that aspect of the Law. They also ignored the woman's right to a formal trial and execution, not merely stoning by a lynch mob. Jesus' views on the Law were well known, and the accusers were probably confident that He would not endorse a death penalty for adultery with no chance for mercy. If He refused to pass any judgment, the woman would be stoned, and He would be tacitly responsible. But if He declared that she should not be stoned, then He could be accused of teaching against the Law.[3]

Write (8:6). At first Jesus does ignore the accusers. Many people have speculated about what Jesus wrote in the dust, but there is no way of knowing. He may have written what He later spoke (8:7); it was customary for Roman judges first to write their sentences and then read them aloud. He may have written something from the Law, such as Exodus 23:1b.[4]

1. What sins do we know the adulteress's accusers committed (8:3-9)?

_____

_____

_____

_____

_____

_____

2. What do Jesus' words in this story reveal about His views on sin and judgment?

_____

_____

_____

_____

_____

_____

3. Put yourself in the place of the woman or her accusers. How did you feel while this scene was going on? What impressions of Jesus were you left with?

_____

_____

_____

_____

_____

Optional Application: Do Jesus' words in 8:10-11 apply to you? If so, how, and what will you do about this? Ask Jesus for a deep conviction that He does not condemn you and that He invites you to abandon your sin. Rely on His promises in 8:31-36 to free you from sin. Consider meditating on some of these verses.

Optional Application: How quick are you to want to throw stones at others? Are you ever like the woman's accusers? Pray about this.

Jesus and the Jews

Who sinned (9:2). Most Jews believed that suffering was the result of one's sin. But the disciples couldn't see how a person could have earned a birth defect. (Some rabbis did cite Genesis 25:22-23 as evidence that one could sin and reap judgment in the womb. Others thought that souls existed before conception and could sin before then. However, these were not widely held views.) They also could not see how it would be fair for the man to suffer for his par-

For Thought and Discussion: a. Is suffering always, sometimes, or never a result of one's own sin (5:14, 9:2-3)? Give evidence for your view. How should this affect the way you deal with sin and suffering in your own life?

b. Is it just for God to let children suffer for the sins of their parents? Is it just for Him to let children reap the benefits of their parents' godliness? Why or why not?

Optional Application: a. Ask God to show you whether your afflictions are the consequences of sins you need to repent of, or whether they are the results of your sins at all. If you feel convicted of sin, confess and know that you are forgiven (1 John 1:9) even if your symptoms do not go away immediately.

b. Ask God to display His work through the afflictions of your life (9:3).

ents' sin (although the rabbis did teach this, and Exodus 20:5 implies it).

_____

4. What wrong ideas about sin are voiced or implied in 7:53–9:41?

8:1-6 _____

_____

_____

_____

_____

8:33 _____

_____

_____

_____

9:2 _____

_____

_____

_____

_____

9:13-16,24 _____

_____

_____

_____

_____

9:34 _____

_____

_____

_____

_____

5. What does Jesus say about sin in these verses?

8:24 _____

_____

_____

_____

8:31-36 _____

_____

_____

_____

_____

_____

8:37-45,47 _____

_____

_____

_____

_____

_____

8:46 _____

_____

_____

9:3 _____

_____

_____

_____

9:41 _____

For Thought and Discussion: If a person lies or desires to kill, what does this reveal about him, and why (8:44-45)?

For Thought and Discussion: What does Jesus say about judgment in 8:15-16,50?

For Thought and Discussion: Why can a person know the truth only if he holds to Jesus' teaching (8:31-32)?

For Further Study:
a. Later groups called "Gnostics" taught that people needed to be set free from ignorance by knowing the truth about their divine origins, about why matter was evil but the spirit was good, and about their divine destiny. Is this the kind of truth Jesus means in 8:32? Explain.
    b. Trace the words *truth* and *true* through John's Gospel, starting with 14:6.

6. Rewrite 8:31-32 in your own words, explaining what Jesus means.

_____

_____

_____

_____

_____

7. On page 30, summarize what 7:53-9:41 reveals about Jesus' identity. Then, summarize the main message of 7:53-9:41 below.

_____

_____

_____

_____

_____

Your response

8. What one insight from lesson eleven seems most relevant to your life?

_____

_____

_____

9. How would you like this truth to affect who you are and what you do?

_____

_____

_____

_____

_____

For Thought and Discussion: Does Jesus glorify Himself in 8:1-9:41? Consider 8:49-50,54 and 8:12,29,58.

10. What practical steps can you take to bring your life more into line with this truth?

_____

_____

_____

_____

_____

11. List any questions you have about this lesson.

_____

_____

_____

_____

For the group

Warm-up. Sin is a key concept in these chapters—indeed, in the whole Bible. So you could ask group members what they think "sin" is. Essentially, the Greek word implies "missing the mark," failing to reach a goal or standard set by God (Romans 3:23). But there is much more to it than that. Sin is a character bent, a moral and mental disease that clouds our perception of reality and cripples us from doing and being what God created us for.

Worship. Thank Jesus for His right judgments and His mercy, His desire that sinners may abandon their sin, hold onto His teaching, and be freed from compulsive sin. Thank Him for using even your afflictions to glorify the Father.

1. Even the most conservative scholars agree that this passage is not an original part of John's Gospel. "It is not attested in the oldest manuscripts, and when it does make its appearance it is sometimes found in other positions, either after v. 36 [7:36], or after v. 44 [7:44], or at the end of this Gospel [probably as an appendix to the four Gospels], or after Luke 21:38. It seems clear enough that those scribes who felt it too important to be lost were not at all sure where to attach it." Furthermore, "the manuscripts which have it do not agree closely." However, "if we cannot feel that this is part of John's Gospel we can feel that the story is true to the character of Jesus. Throughout the history of the church it has been held that, whoever wrote it, this little story is authentic. It rings true." Therefore, we recognize in this account the authority of Holy Scripture and include it in a study of John's Gospel. It certainly fits thematically with Jesus' teaching on sin and judgment in this section. See Morris, pages 882-883. Brown, volume 29, pages 335-336, agrees with Morris's conclusion.
2. Morris, page 885.
3. Morris, pages 886-888; compare Brown, volume 29, page 337.
4. Brown, volume 29, pages 333-334; Morris, pages 888-889.

JOHN 10:1-42

The Good Shepherd

The Pharisees have rejected Jesus as a sinner, thrown His new disciple out of the synagogue, and denied their own blindness (9:24,34,40). In response, Jesus tells a parable about how a good shepherd differs from Israel's current shepherds, who are no better than hirelings or even thieves. John puts together two discourses—10:1-21, which apparently took place shortly after the healing in chapter 9, and 10:22-42, which occurred two months later. Read 10:1-42.

Discourse after Tabernacles (10:1-21)

Gate (10:1-3,7,9). Among the Arabs today, the sheep are sometimes kept in an enclosure with walls, partial roofing, and one opening. At night, the shepherd lies down in that open space so the sheep can't wander and wolves can't get in without crossing him.[1] In this sense, the shepherd is the gate. However, John 10:3 seems to envision a larger sheep pen in which several flocks are kept; a *watchman* guards the pen, which has a real gate. Jesus plays with the image of the gate from many angles.

Shepherd (10:2,11). In the Old Testament, God is often described as Israel's Shepherd (Genesis 49:24; Psalm 23:1-2, 78:52). Because the patriarchs, Moses, and David were all shepherds, the word came to be used of "the rulers of God's people. . . . Impious kings were scathingly denounced as wicked shepherds"[2] (1 Kings 22:17, Jeremiah 10:21). In Ezekiel 34, God accuses the shepherds (rulers) who have plundered and neglected the weak, sick, and straying. "So they were scattered because there was no shepherd, and . . . they became food for all the wild animals" (Ezekiel 34:5). God declares that He will rescue His flock from the wicked shepherds and will shepherd it Himself. He will bring back the lost, heal the wounded, and strengthen the weak. (Note: Our word *pastor* is simply the Latin for "shepherd.")

Voice (10:3-5,16). Palestinian shepherds often have pet names for each of their sheep. When two flocks spend a night together, the shepherds sort them out by standing at a distance and calling each sheep by name. The sheep do know their names and their shepherd's voice.[3]

Hired hand (10:12). By Jewish law, a hired man was required to defend the sheep with his life if one wolf attacked, but he was not responsible for any damage done by two wolves attacking simultaneously. He could flee without penalty.[4]

1. Below, write down the characteristics of the true or good shepherd, and explain what each one tells you about Jesus.

   10:2,7 _____

   _____

   _____

   _____

   _____

   _____

   10:3-4,14 _____

   _____

   _____

10:10 _____

_____

_____

_____

_____

_____

_____

10:11 _____

_____

_____

_____

_____

For Thought and Discussion: a. By what means were the priests and Pharisees trying to enter the sheep pen, other than by the gate who is Jesus (10:1,7-8)?

b. By what means are various modern impostors trying to enter?

2. a. By contrast, how may thieves and robbers (false shepherds) be recognized (10:1-10)?

_____

_____

_____

_____

_____

_____

b. Give an example of how a leader (a Pharisee, a priest, a modern pastor or preacher) might do these things.

_____

_____

_____

For Thought and Discussion: How can modern leaders follow the example of 10:2-4,11,14-15?

Optional Application: Do you know the difference between the good shepherd's voice and the voices of impostors (10:3-5,14)? What is the evidence in your life? How can you grow better able to distinguish the good shepherd's voice from clever imitations?

For Thought and Discussion: a. What does Jesus mean by saying that whoever enters by Him "will come in and go out, and find pasture" (10:9)?
  b. What is "life . . . to the full" (10:10)? What are its characteristics?

3. a. How does a hired hand behave, and why (10:12-14)?

b. How might a modern pastor do this?

4. Jesus makes two "I am" statements in chapter 10. What is He claiming about Himself and His identity by calling Himself . . .

the gate (10:7-9)? _____

the good shepherd (10:11)? _____

112

5. a. What happens to the sheep who know and follow the good shepherd (10:3-4,9-10,27-29)?

_____

_____

_____

_____

_____

_____

b. What is involved for you in enjoying that kind of relationship with Jesus?

_____

_____

_____

_____

_____

_____

6. What goal for His mission is Jesus describing in 10:16?

_____

_____

_____

_____

_____

7. Why is 10:18 a crucial truth about Jesus?

_____

_____

_____

_____

For Thought and Discussion: What is implied by the fact that Jesus and His sheep know each other *just as* He and His Father know each other (10:14-15)?

For Thought and Discussion: Why is it important that there is only "one flock and one shepherd" (10:16)? What are the implications for you, your town, and other Christians you know?

a. Observe the various reactions to Jesus in 10:19-21. How are they like and unlike reactions you have heard?

b. How can 10:21 guide you in demonstrating to your friends why Jesus must be God, not a madman?

Optional Application: Are you following the good shepherd as closely as a sheep would (10:4,27)? How could you improve in this area? What are the implications for your priorities and choices?

Discourse at the Dedication (10:22-42)

Feast of Dedication (10:22). Hanukkah—an eight-day feast in late November or December. From 167-164 BC, the Syrians profaned the Temple by setting up an idol on the altar. On Chislev 25 in 164 BC, "Judas Maccabeus drove out the Syrians, built a new altar, and rededicated the Temple."[5] The Feast of Dedication commemorated the reconsecration of the Temple and altar.

I did tell you (10:25). He had never told them outright that He was the Christ, and He did not say plainly "Yes" now, for the Jews so misunderstood what the Messiah was that the answer would have misled them. But had they been paying attention to the obvious meanings of His signs, His actions, His teaching, and His statements like 8:58, the Jews would not have had to ask whether He was the Christ. He had been saying so with every word and act.

Hand (10:28-29). Jesus gave more of an answer than the Jews bargained for when they asked whether He was the Christ. He intimately linked "my hand" with "my Father's hand," then said, *I and the Father are one* (10:30).

8. Some people still think "one" in 10:30 means "one in will" rather than "one in essence." They say that Jesus was not claiming equal divinity with the Father. How did the Jews interpret Jesus' statement (10:31,33)?

114

Your Law (10:34). Jesus is referring to the Jewish Scriptures in general, not to the books of Moses, since He is quoting a psalm.

Gods (10:34). In Psalm 82, God addresses the rulers and judges of Israel as "gods." This was a common concept in the Near East—"rulers and judges, as deputies of the heavenly King, could be given the honorific title 'god.'"[6]

9. What is Jesus' point in 10:34-36?

_____

_____

_____

_____

_____

10. As before, what is the evidence that Jesus' audacious claims are true, not blasphemous (10:37-38)?

_____

_____

_____

_____

Your response

11. Summarize Jesus' teaching in chapter 10. (Also, make any notes about Jesus' identity on page 30.)

_____

_____

_____

For Thought and Discussion: Consider what Jesus does when threatened with imminent death (10:31-32,39). What do you learn about His character?

For Thought and Discussion: Jesus says of an insignificant bit of a psalm, "the Scripture cannot be broken" (10:35). What does this imply about His view of the Scriptures?

_____

_____

12. What one truth from 10:1-42 would you like to concentrate on for application this week?

_____

_____

_____

_____

13. What implications does this truth have for your life? (How would you like it to affect you? How do you fall short in this area?)

_____

_____

_____

_____

14. What steps can you take to begin making this truth more a part of your life?

_____

_____

_____

_____

15. List any questions you have about chapter 10.

_____

_____

_____

_____

For the group

Warm-up. Ask the group what the idea of a shepherd suggests to them.

Questions. The parables in chapter 10 are not as easy as they seem because Jesus keeps using the images in different ways. At one point He compares Himself to the gate, which the true shepherd uses but robbers bypass. Then He calls Himself the shepherd. Don't worry about how He can be both the gate and the shepherd who enters it.

Worship. Praise Jesus as the gate—the one door to good pasture and abundant life. Praise Him as the shepherd who calls His sheep by name and lays down His life for them. Praise Him for having complete control of His life, both to lay it down and to take it up again.

I and the Father Are One

When the Church was coming to understand the Trinity in the early centuries, John 10:30 was considered a key. Some people thought "one" meant "one Person." They said that Father, Son, and Spirit were simply modes of one Person ("God acted as Father in the creation, the Son in redemption and Holy Spirit in prophecy and sanctification"[7]). But the word is neuter—"one thing." Furthermore, as Augustine explained it, "are" refuted this idea of modes of one Person.

On the other hand, some believed that the Son was a created being who was not fully God. They said that "one" meant simply "one in will and purpose." Augustine insisted that "one" meant "one in essence" or "one in kind." This word refuted those who made Christ less than fully God.[8] The mystery of the Trinity is that Father, Son, and Spirit are three distinct Persons who are each fully God and together are the One God. They are not three Gods, three aspects of God, or three parts of God. Nor are the Son and Spirit less fully God than the Father.

---

1. Brown, volume 29, page 397.
2. Morris, page 507, note 30.
3. Morris, page 502, note 17; Brown, volume 29, page 385.

4. Morris, page 511.
5. Brown, volume 29, page 402; citing 1 Maccabees 1:54, 4:41-61; 2 Maccabees 6:1-7. The Maccabees are books that were part of the Jewish Scriptures among the Greek-speaking Jews of Jesus' day but were later excluded from the canon. They are regarded as historically helpful but not divinely inspired.
6. *The NIV Study Bible*, page 873. See also Morris, pages 525-526, note 92.
7. W. H. C. Frend, *The Early Church* (Philadelphia: Fortress Press, 1982), page 77.
8. Brown, volume 29, page 403.

JOHN 11:1-57

Lazarus Raised

When the Jews asked Jesus if He was the Christ, His answer would have led to a lynching if God had allowed it (10:24,30-31,39). That was in December. Afterward, Jesus crossed the Jordan and ministered in Perea for a couple of months (10:40-42). He knew that the next time He set foot in Jerusalem would be His last. As winter was passing, an urgent message came from close friends less than two miles from Jerusalem (11:18). Read about the effects of that message in 11:1-57.

For Further Study:
Read about Mary and Martha in Luke 10:38-42.

The raising (11:1-44)

Poured perfume (11:2). This incident did not happen until later (12:3), but John's first readers must have been familiar with the story.

Four days (11:17). "There was a Jewish belief that the soul stays near the grave for three days, hoping to be able to return to the body. But on the fourth day it sees decomposition setting in and leaves it finally." After that, there was no hope of resuscitation by natural means.[1]

Weeping (11:33). "The word signifies a loud weeping, a wailing. It was the habit of the day to express grief in a noisy, rather unrestrained fashion."[2] By contrast, *wept* (11:35) is a different verb that denotes a more quiet shedding of tears.[3]

119

For Thought and Discussion: Compare 11:4 to 9:3. Is this a frequent truth about affliction? Or is this principle unique to Jesus' ministry? Give reasons for your view.

Deeply moved in spirit and troubled (11:33). This phrase could imply anger—anger against death, which is the effect of man's fall and Satan's evil work. Or, it may mean distress that the mourners, even His dear friends, did not understand what He had come to do about death. It could also mean that Jesus was identifying with His friends, feeling their grief, gathering their pain into Himself. Finally, it may imply that working this miracle cost Jesus something.[4]

1. Why do you think John stresses Jesus' love for Lazarus and his sisters in this account (11:3,5,36)?

_____

_____

_____

_____

_____

2. Despite His love for Lazarus, why doesn't Jesus go immediately when He learns of the sickness (11:4-6,14-15,25-26,41-42)?

_____

_____

_____

_____

3. a. Jesus' disciples warn Him that going to Bethany, less than two miles from Jerusalem, is highly dangerous (11:8). What is the point Jesus' makes in response (11:9-10)?

_____

_____

_____

_____

_____

b. What does Jesus' response tell you about His character and priorities (11:9-11)?

_____

_____

_____

_____

_____

c. How is this relevant to your circumstances?

_____

_____

_____

_____

_____

For Thought and Discussion: What attitude does Thomas express in 11:16? What is admirable and flawed about this attitude?

For Thought and Discussion: Why do you think Jesus was deeply moved and wept (11:33-35)?

4. The raising of Lazarus is the last and greatest of Jesus' signs before His own resurrection. What does it reveal about . . .

Jesus' (and the Father's) character, personality, and values (see especially 11:14-15,25-26,33-35, 40-42)?

_____

_____

_____

_____

_____

Jesus' mission? _____

_____

_____

Jesus' identity (see especially 11:25-27,41-44)?

_____

_____

_____

_____

5. What implications does this event have for
   Mary, Martha, and you (11:25-27,40-42)?

_____

_____

_____

_____

The plot (11:45-57)

The Romans will come (11:48). Popular disorder
was one thing the Romans did not tolerate in
their provinces, and Judea was already seething
with discontent ready to explode. The Roman
authorities were on edge to stamp out any spark
of revolt. If Jesus rallied the crowds with a claim
to kingship, the Romans would act. They would
destroy the Jews' holy ***place***—the Temple, or
perhaps the city—and might even massacre and
deport the population. Ironically, this is exactly
what happened in 70 AD after the Jews revolted
from Rome. Killing Jesus did not prevent it.

High priest that year (11:49). The high priesthood
was supposed to be a lifelong office. However,
the Romans had claimed the right to depose

and appoint high priests, and they did so fairly often. *Caiaphas* was the official high priest from 18 to 36 AD. Nevertheless, many Jews did not fully accept Rome's right to supersede God's Law. They continued to regard Annas, the father-in-law of Caiaphas, as the true high priest because he had held office until the Romans replaced him in 15 AD, and he was still alive (18:13).

Ephraim (11:54). If most archaeologists are right, this village was about twelve miles northeast of Jerusalem—not very far away, but in a lonely, mountainous place on the edge of the desert.[5]

Ceremonial cleansing (11:55). "Ceremonial defilement disqualified a man from keeping the Passover [Leviticus 7:21, Numbers 9:6]. Depending on what was involved the rites for purification might last as long as a week so that, with large numbers involved, it might be well to come to the city early."[6]

Optional
Application: Do pre-conceptions ever cloud your assessment of evidence about God's deeds? Pray about this.

6. Observe how the Jewish leaders reacted to the news of the stupendous miracle in Bethany (11:45-48). What was wrong with their values and their approach to the facts?

_____

_____

_____

_____

_____

7. a. What do you think Caiaphas meant in 11:50?

_____

_____

_____

_____

_____

123

b. What deeper meaning does John discern in Caiaphas's words (11:51-52)?

_____

_____

_____

_____

_____

Your response

8. Add any thoughts from chapter 11 to your list on page 30.

9. What one truth from 11:1-57 would you like to take to heart this week?

_____

_____

_____

_____

_____

10. How is this truth relevant to your life? How would you like it to affect what you do?

_____

_____

_____

_____

_____

11. What action can you take with God's help to begin putting this into practice and making it a habit?

_____

_____

_____

_____

_____

_____

12. List any questions you have about chapter 11.

_____

_____

_____

_____

For the group

Warm-up. Ask everyone to think of a time when he or she lost a loved one. Ask each person to remember how he or she felt, especially about God, at that time. You might give one or two people a chance to describe their feelings.

Questions.

Worship. Praise Jesus for being the resurrection and the life, for guaranteeing that death cannot overcome those who believe in Him. Praise Him for His mighty power over death and all evils in your own lives.

1. Morris, page 546.
2. Morris, page 555.
3. Morris, page 558.
4. Morris, pages 556-558.
5. Brown, volume 29, page 441.
6. Morris, page 569, note 111.

JOHN 12:1-50

The Hour Comes

Jerusalem and the villages round about are buzzing with the news of how Jesus raised a man after four days in the tomb. Pilgrims from Galilee are pouring into the Holy City and adding their own testimony about the teacher from Nazareth. Everyone has the same question: Is this the Messiah, the King who will deliver Israel from Roman oppression and bring the golden age of peace and prosperity? But such speculations must be whispered, for the Sanhedrin regards Jesus as a criminal and has decreed that to conceal His whereabouts is a punishable offense (11:55-57).

Jesus has not been seen since the miracle, and many doubt that He will dare to appear in Jerusalem for the Passover. This is the crucial moment: Will Jesus defy the Sanhedrin and claim His throne, or will He retreat? But neither the plotters nor the crowds understand Jesus' heart. Read 12:1-50.

Anointing in Bethany (12:1-8)

Six days before the Passover (12:1). Jesus arrived on Friday evening, and the *dinner* (12:2) was a sabbath meal.

A pint of pure nard (12:3). A large amount of very expensive scented oil. It was customary to pour such oil on a guest's head on a festive occasion to honor him. To pour it on *Jesus' feet* was an

127

For Thought and Discussion: a. Are you inclined to feel that Mary's act was an extravagant waste of what could have been spent on the poor? Why or why not?
b. Was this a unique situation, or does it have relevance for our priorities? Explain.
c. Judas's pretended altruism and compassion was really selfishness. Do you or other Christians ever fall into this trap? If so, how?

act of extreme humility, since the feet symbolized lowliness (recall 1:27). Only a menial slave would attend to someone's feet. Moreover, Mary *wiped his feet with her hair*, which Jews considered to be a woman's glory (1 Corinthians 11:15). "A Jewish lady never unbound her hair in public. That apparently was a mark of loose morals. But Mary did not stop to calculate public reaction."[1]

Those present would have interpreted Mary's act as signifying devotion, humility, and above all, festivity. But Jesus discerned the meaning of anointing a body for *burial* (12:7). It was the Jewish custom to wrap bodies in linen with scented oils and spices (19:40). Jesus knew He was the Messiah, the "Anointed One," but His mind was on anointing not for kingship or celebration but for burial.

A year's wages (12:5). Three hundred denarii was about a year's wages for a manual laborer.[2]

1. How do you interpret Mary's feelings and reasons for what she does in 12:3?

_____

_____

_____

_____

2. What attitudes about Himself, His mission, and His friends' priorities does Jesus express in 12:7-8?

_____

_____

_____

_____

128

Triumphal entry (12:9-19)

The next day (12:12). Sunday.

The chief priests (12:10). They are panicking—one death was enough before (11:50), but now two will be necessary to protect priestly control. The priests are especially hostile to Lazarus because as Sadducees they reject the Pharisaic doctrine of resurrection. Lazarus is a living example of what they assert to be impossible.[3]

The great crowd (12:12). These were "the country people who were coming up to Jerusalem for the feast, probably most of them from Galilee."[4] Many of these had seen and heard of Jesus' works in Galilee, so when they heard that He was nearby and coming to the feast, and when they learned of a miracle even more amazing than any they had seen, they went to meet Him.

They had tried earlier to proclaim Him the Messiah, but He had resisted (6:15). This time He accepted their acclamation, and they went wild.

Palm branches (12:13). These had "political overtones"[5]—they were carried when the Temple was liberated from the Syrians in 164 BC and when the Jerusalem citadel was retaken from enemies in 142 BC. They symbolized kingship, victory, and nationalism. The crowds **went out to meet** Jesus—"This was the normal Greek expression used to describe the joyful reception of Hellenistic sovereigns into a city."[6] They shouted **Hosanna** (O save!), a term of praise to God and of greeting to kings (2 Samuel 14:4, 2 Kings 6:26, Psalm 118:25).[7] They quoted the acclamation for the Messiah in Psalm 118:26— **Blessed is he who comes in the name of the Lord.** They added another title, **the King of Israel** to make their meaning explicit.

Donkey (12:14-15). Faced with this tumult, Jesus sent His disciples to fetch a donkey that had never been ridden (Luke 19:29-36). Riding into Jerusalem on a donkey was a prophetic action that expressed Jesus' idea of messiahship in response to the crowd's nationalism. A warrior

For Thought and Discussion: What do you think John wants us to learn from the scene in 12:1-8? What points does the scene make about Jesus and how people respond to Him?

Optional Application: Instead of changing their doctrine, the priests want to murder the witnesses and destroy the evidence. Are you ever like that?

129

For Further Study:
a. Study Zechariah
9:9-13 to see the
context of the kind of
King Jesus was claim-
ing to be. Notice the
references to "right-
eous," "gentle,"
"peace to the
nations," "the blood
of my covenant," and
"free your prisoners."
b. The beginning
of John 12:15 recalls
Zephaniah 3:14-17.
Read that passage,
and observe who "the
King of Israel" is,
what His mission is,
and why Zion need no
longer be afraid. What
sort of King is Jesus?

**For Thought and
Discussion:** How did
the Jewish leaders
react to the reception
the crowds gave
Jesus (12:9-11,19)?

would ride a warhorse, but a king on a mission
of peace would ride an unbroken (ritually clean)
donkey.[8] Jesus was purposely fulfilling Zechariah 9:9, a prophecy of the Messiah.

His disciples did not understand (12:16). They perceived that Jesus was at last claiming to be the
Messiah, but like the crowds, they did not
understand what Jesus was saying about what
messiahship meant. They, too, saw only the
nationalism and victory.

3. When the Galileans tried to proclaim Jesus
King, He refused (6:15). But at this Passover,
He chose to ride into Jerusalem on a royal donkey amid public acclaim. Why do you think He
accepted the acclaim this time?

_____

_____

_____

_____

_____

4. What impresses you most about the scene in
12:12-19? (For instance, what details strike you
as most significant or personally relevant? Why
is the scene important? What do you think John
wants to teach or reinforce to his readers? How
does the scene make you feel?)

_____

_____

_____

_____

_____

_____

_____

A prediction of death (12:20-36)

The Synoptics include many of Jesus' words and acts after entering Jerusalem in triumph. (See, for example, Luke 19:41–21:38.) But John records only a few items to climax Jesus' public ministry.

Greeks (12:20). These were Gentiles who had abandoned pagan gods and come to worship the God of Israel at the feast. They are not called proselytes, so they were probably not circumcised. There is evidence that hundreds of Gentiles across the Empire found the morality and monotheism of Judaism appealing, although they did not care for the rules, especially circumcision, required of full converts. "Greeks" does not imply that they came from Greece. There were many "Greeks" (Gentiles who spoke Greek) in Galilee and across the Jordan.

These Gentiles did not want just to *see* (12:21) in the sense of glimpsing Him in the crowd. They wanted to see Him in the sense of getting to know Him in some conversation.

---

5. John never does tell us whether the Greeks got to see Jesus. He only records Jesus' response. What did the coming of the Gentiles prompt Jesus to talk about (12:23-28)?

_____

_____

_____

_____

_____

6. Why do you think their coming signaled to Jesus that the hour of His glory had arrived (12:23)?

_____

_____

For Thought and Discussion: Give some examples of good and bad self-hatred.

Optional Application: What kind of dying do you need to go through in order to bear fruit (12:24)?

7. The "hour" was the moment for both Jesus and the Father to be glorified (12:23,27-28). What events were going to glorify the Father and the Son (12:24,30-33)?

8. Why did these events, which appeared to be defeat and humiliation, actually glorify the Father and the Son?

Life (12:25). The first two instances of "life" in this verse are *psyche*—one's physical life or one's self. The last instance is *zoe*—the life that comes from God, the only kind that can exist in eternity. *Loves . . . hates* is a typically Semitic way of expressing contrasts drastically and vividly. To love one's life/self, to be wrapped up in self-fulfillment, self-actualization, self-enjoyment—this is selfishness. To hate one's life (compared to God and others) is self-sacrifice that leads to eternal life.[9]

9. Rewrite 12:24-26 in your own words.

_____

_____

_____

_____

_____

10. Jesus says that what is true for Him is true for
His servant. In what specific ways is 12:24-26
relevant to you?

  a. In what ways do you show that you love your
  life wrongly (12:25)? (Ask God to show you.)

  _____

  _____

  _____

  _____

  b. In what ways are you showing proper indif-
  ference to your own life?

  _____

  _____

  _____

  _____

  c. Where is Jesus? Where do you need to be in
  order to be where He is (12:26)?

  _____

  _____

  _____

For Thought and Discussion: Does "they could not believe" (12:39) mean that the Jews had no free will to believe? Why or why not?

11. Recall the meaning of light from earlier in this Gospel (1:9, 3:19-21, 8:12). What is Jesus saying in 12:35-36?

_____

_____

_____

_____

_____

Sons of (12:36). A Semitic idiom for one who is "characterized by the quality in question."[10]

Summary (12:37-50)

12. According to 12:37-41, why did almost none of the Jews believe in Jesus, despite His signs that pointed to His identity and mission?

_____

_____

_____

_____

_____

Saw Jesus' glory (12:41). Isaiah saw the glory of the Lord (Isaiah 6:3) and foresaw the rejection, death, and exaltation of Jesus (Isaiah 52:13-53:12).

Study Skill—Hebrew Thought
It is important for us to remember that most of the writers of the Bible came from a largely
(continued on page 135)

(continued from page 134)
oriental culture and thought like Jews. We in the West are taught to think with the logic developed by the Greeks. This logic says, for instance, that contradictions are impossible. The Hebrew mind, by contrast, assumes that contradictions and paradoxes do coexist, so it has no trouble holding seemingly contradictory truths in tension. Western minds resist paradoxes, so we try to reason them out logically. Our debates about predestination and free will are prime examples of this effort. The Jews knew that God was supreme, so everything that happened must be at least indirectly caused by Him. Yet, they knew that He had given people freedom to make moral choices for which they were responsible. God caused hard hearts, yet men chose hard hearts (Exodus 8:15, 9:12). Because their Hebrew minds could accept this tension, the biblical writers did not reason it out for us. We need to learn to think like Hebrews if we are to understand the Bible.

Optional Application: Does 12:42-43 describe you in any way? If so, repent and ask God what you need to start doing differently.

13. Many prominent people did privately believe that Jesus was the Christ. What priorities kept them from confessing their faith publicly (12:42-43)?

_____

_____

_____

_____

Cried out (12:44). This suggests that Jesus declared these words in public (compare 7:37, 11:43), probably before He "hid himself" (12:36) from the Jews. John apparently positioned Jesus' final appeal to His people here as a fitting summary and conclusion to Jesus' public ministry. Hereafter, Jesus will not appear to the crowds until He is crucified.

135

14. What does Jesus say in His final appeal
    (12:44-50) about . . .

    His identity and relationship to the Father?

    _____

    _____

    _____

    _____

    His mission? _____

    _____

    _____

    _____

    those who reject Him and His words? _____

    _____

    _____

    _____

Your response

15. What one insight from chapter 12 seems most
    personally relevant to you right now?

    _____

    _____

    _____

    _____

    _____

16. How do you fall short or need to grow in this
    area?

    _____

    _____

    _____

_____

_____

17. What can you do to begin conforming your life
more to God's will in this area?

_____

_____

_____

_____

18. List any questions you have about 12:1-50.

_____

_____

_____

_____

For the group

Warm-up. Ask, "What is the most extravagant thing
you ever did to show someone that you loved him or
her?" Let everyone think for a while, then let one or
two people answer. This may help the group relate
to what Mary did when she poured outrageously
expensive oil over Jesus' feet.

Questions. Question 4 is a good type of open-ended
question for groups that do not care for narrowly
directive questions. If it works well for you, use it
often when you discuss passages. If it leaves the
group uncertain about what to say, ask some more
specific questions about the scene.

Question 10 is a pointed application question
designed to help you wrestle personally with Jesus'
words. You can focus on it if it seems to be the area
you need to work on. Or, you can cover it lightly
and concentrate on another area for application.
Just be sure that you each face something for personal challenge.

Worship. Praise Jesus as He who comes in the name of the Lord, the King of Israel, the King who comes with a mission of peace, the Anointed One who is anointed for death and burial, He who glorified the Father and Himself by His death, He who came as light, He who spoke and acted as the Father commanded, He who reveals the Father. Ask Him to help you believe in Him, keep His words, love Him more than your lives, and go where He goes.

1. Morris, pages 576-577.
2. Morris, page 578.
3. Morris, page 582.
4. Morris, page 583.
5. Brown, volume 29, page 461.
6. Brown, volume 29, pages 461-462.
7. Brown, volume 29, pages 457, 462.
8. Morris, page 587; I. H. Marshall, *The Gospel of Luke* (Grand Rapids, Michigan: William B. Eerdmans Publishing Company, 1978), page 712.
9. Morris, page 594; Brown, volume 29, page 467.
10. Morris, page 601.

JOHN 13:1-38

Love and Betrayal

On Sunday the crowds hailed Jesus as King while He rode royally into Jerusalem and up to the Temple. But instead of claiming His throne and launching the war of liberation, Jesus again drove the merchants from the Temple and sat down to teach (Luke 19:45-21:38). The crowds were disappointed but the Sanhedrin was not appeased, and one of Jesus' closest disciples was fed up. Jesus had sealed His own fate.

By Wednesday He had nothing more to say to the crowds—they had judged themselves by their attitudes toward Him. But He had much more to say to His twelve core disciples and little time to say it. On Thursday evening the thirteen men gathered around a meal; only Jesus knew what would happen before dawn. Read 13:1-38.

For Thought and Discussion: How does John describe the torture and death Jesus was about to undergo (13:1,3)? What does this tell you about John's (and Jesus') attitude toward those sufferings?

Footwashing (13:1-17)

1. How would you describe Jesus' attitude in 13:1-5?

_____

_____

_____

_____

_____

139

For Thought and Discussion: Some Christian groups literally wash each others' feet periodically. What are some potentially good and bad results of doing this once or as a periodic practice? How could the good results be achieved without the bad ones?

2. How is the statement, "the Father had put all things under his power" (13:3) consistent with the fact that Jesus is about to be arrested, tortured, and executed?

_____

_____

_____

_____

_____

Iscariot (13:2). This probably means "man of Keri-oth [a town in southern Judea]."[1] "Judas was thus the only one of the Twelve who was not a Galilean."[2] He may have had sympathies with the Judean hierarchy; he may have finally admitted to himself that Jesus was not the Messiah he wanted; none of the Gospels tell us more about his motives than that *the devil had . . . prompted* him to betray Jesus for money (Luke 22:1-6, John 13:2).

Took off his outer clothing (13:4). "Jesus stripped to a loin cloth, just like a slave."[3]

Wash his disciples' feet (13:5). This was a menial task (recall the symbolism of feet from 1:27 and 12:3). People went barefoot or in sandals, so their feet got muddy and dusty outdoors. Guests' feet were usually washed on arrival at the host's home—certainly before the meal—by a servant, but Jesus did it in the midst of the meal to make a point.

3. Why do you think Peter objects to what Jesus is doing (13:6-8)?

_____

_____

_____

_____

Only . . . his feet (13:10). A person going to a feast at that time bathed at home so that when he arrived he needed only to have his feet washed for him to be entirely clean.[4]

4. Why does Jesus insist that Peter needs Jesus to wash his feet, although he doesn't need a full bath (13:8-10)? What point is Jesus making?

_____

_____

_____

_____

_____

5. The footwashing has several lessons for the disciples. What lessons or meanings does Jesus state in . . .

13:8-10? _____

_____

_____

_____

13:12-17? _____

_____

_____

_____

_____

For Thought and Discussion: How does the footwashing illustrate the meaning of the Cross?

For Thought and Discussion: Think of as many ways as possible in which modern Christians can wash each other's feet.

Optional Application:
a. Whose feet do you need to wash and how?

b. Who washes your feet? How are you showing your gratitude for this?

c. Ask God to make you quick to wash others' feet with joy and love. Ask Him to make you willing to let others wash your feet.

d. Meditate on 13:14,17.

Messenger (13:16). See the note on "sent" on page 55. The word here is *apostolos*, suggesting the Jewish *shaliach*, the one sent with the authority and obligation to do what the sender would

Optional Application: a. Jesus knew who He was, where He was from, where He was going, and what power and authority He had (13:3). Do you fully know these about yourself?

b. Why does knowing these things about yourself make it possible for you to wash others' feet without pride or resentment?

c. Ask God to enable you to know who you are.

Optional Application: What are the implications of 13:20 for your decisions and priorities?

do. Notice that what is done to the *shaliach* is regarded as done to the sender (13:20).

6. In your judgment, to what extent do 13:16 and 13:20 describe the authority and mission of only a few leaders like the apostles? To what extent do these verses describe your authority and mission? (Give reasons for your view.)

_____

_____

_____

_____

_____

_____

Judas' betrayal predicted (13:18-30)

Reclining (13:23). This was the customary position for the Passover meal.[5] "The usual arrangement . . . was to have a series of couches each for three persons arranged in a U round the table. The host, or the most important person reclined in the centre of the chief couch placed at the junction of the two arms of the U. The guests reclined with their heads towards the table and their feet stretched out obliquely away from it. They leaned on the left elbow, which meant that the right hand was free to secure food. The place of honor was to the left of, and thus slightly behind the principal person. The second place was to his right, and the guest there would have his head on the breast of the host. Plainly this was the position occupied by the beloved disciple."[6]

We might have thought that Peter would have the place of honor. But he seems to have been too far from Jesus to whisper a question himself (13:24), and he could scarcely have motioned to John if he was behind Jesus, who was behind John. Judas was near enough to

142

Jesus to receive a piece of food from him (13:26), so he may have had the place of honor. He was the group's treasurer (12:6, 13:29), an important role, and Jesus may have been making a subtle last appeal to him.[7]

7. Why did Jesus predict the betrayal to His disciples, but in a veiled manner (10:18; 13:3,19)?

_____

_____

_____

_____

Peter's denial predicted (13:31-38)

Now that Judas has gone to fetch the temple guard, Jesus has only a few hours to say His parting words to His dearest friends. He begins with a teaching that has been implicit in the whole training of His disciples, but that He only now makes explicit (13:34-35). We will look at this command again along with 15:12-13 in lesson sixteen. In chapter 13 Peter completely ignores the new commandment because he is so aghast that Jesus intends to go somewhere without His disciples (13:33-36).

8. What is ironic about Peter's conviction that he will lay down his life for his Master (13:37-38; compare 10:11,15; 18:8-18,25-27)?

_____

_____

_____

_____

9. Knowing what Judas and Peter are about to do, Jesus gives His "new commandment." Compare John 13:34 to Leviticus 19:18. What is new about 13:34?

_____

Optional Application: Have you ever been betrayed or let down by a friend? If so, compare the way you felt and acted to what Jesus felt and did about Judas (13:18-30, Luke 22:47-48) and Peter (John 13:37-38, 21:15-19; Luke 22:31-32). What might Jesus have done if He had been bitter about either man?

For Thought and Discussion: How is it ironic that Jesus gave His new commandment (13:34-35, 15:12-13) in the midst of knowing what Judas and Peter were about to do?

Optional Application: Are you at all like Peter in 13:36-38? How accurate is your own assessment of your devotion to Jesus? Pray about this.

Optional Application: How has Jesus loved you? How can you love someone this week with this same love?

For Thought and Discussion: Why do you think actively loving other Christians is such an effective way to evangelize non-Christians (13:35)?

10. How does the footwashing help to explain this commandment?

_____

_____

_____

_____

_____

11. Why is this command so crucial for Christians to keep (13:35)?

_____

_____

_____

_____

Your response

12. What one truth from 13:1-38 would you like to concentrate on for application this week?

_____

_____

_____

_____

13. How do you fall short in this area? How would you like this truth to affect your life?

_____

_____

_____

_____

_____

14. What practical steps can you take toward
    cooperating with God in achieving this end?

_____

_____

_____

_____

15. List any questions you have about chapter 13.

_____

_____

_____

For the group

Warm-up. Ask everyone to remember the most
menial or unpleasant act of service that someone
has done for him or her recently. Or, have everyone
think of the most menial thing he or she has done
for someone else recently.

Questions. Focus on the footwashing. Be sure the
group understands both aspects of it: how it is
something Jesus uniquely does for us, and how it is
something we must do for each other. When you
think you understand what Jesus was saying
through the footwashing, list together as many ways
of washing one another's feet as you can. In particular, look for ways of washing other group members'
feet. Discuss "the new commandment" and its connection with the footwashing.

Worship. Praise Jesus for washing you wholly so
that you need only to have Him wash your feet peri-

145

odically. Thank Him for the ultimate act of humility He performed to wash you. Ask Him to show you how to wash others' feet. Praise Him for embracing betrayal by His friends without bitterness.

The Date of Passover

According to the official calendar of the temple authorities, the beginning of Passover was apparently Friday evening in that year. The Jewish leaders had not yet eaten the Passover on Friday morning when they were having Jesus condemned (18:28). They wanted Jesus executed before the Sabbath and the festival week began, because trying and executing a criminal during the feast was irreligious. Thus it came about that Jesus died on Friday afternoon shortly before the Passover lambs were slaughtered in the Temple, graphically fulfilling John the Baptist's prophecy in 1:29.

However, the Synoptics make it clear that the meal Jesus ate with His disciples on Thursday evening was the Passover (Luke 22:7-13). Jesus was determined to eat this Passover with His friends before His death (Luke 22:15-16). Perhaps because He knew He must be arrested before the official Passover, He seems to have celebrated it a day ahead. Several sects, including the community at Qumran, disagreed with the official calendar and routinely ate their Passover a day or so before the official date. They had to do without a lamb (the Gospels mention no lamb at this meal) because a lamb could be eaten only if it was slaughtered by the priests in the Temple on the day they recognized. But Jews who were anywhere but Jerusalem also had to do without lambs, so this was no great hardship.[8]

1. Brown, volume 29, page 298.
2. Morris, page 391, note 161.
3. Morris, page 615, note 15.
4. Morris, page 618.
5. Brown, volume 29A, page 551.
6. Morris, pages 625-626.
7. Morris, page 626.
8. This is the explanation given in Morris, pages 774-785, for why the Synoptics and John seem to differ as to the date of Passover.

JOHN 14:1-16:33

Parting Words: 1

Jesus knows that less than twenty-four hours remain before His death, perhaps less than six until His arrest. The eleven men sharing His last meal are His dearest friends and more: they are the core of those who will carry on His mission when He is gone. In these few hours, Jesus sets aside His own anguish in order to prepare His team for His departure.

These final discourses contain some of Jesus' most profound teaching. Because He returns to the same topics over and over, weaving them together, this lesson asks you to read through 14:1-16:33 and observe what Jesus says about nine major topics. In lesson seventeen you will look more closely at certain parts of these discourses.

1. What would you say is the main point Jesus wants to get across in each chapter?

   14:1-31 _____

   _____

   _____

   _____

   15:1-27 _____

   _____

   _____

For Thought and Discussion: How much of what is said about the Spirit in these chapters could be (or is) said about Jesus? What does this tell you about the relationship between Jesus and the Spirit?

16:1-33 _____

_____

_____

_____

_____

Rooms (14:2). The KJV says "mansions" after the Latin *mansiones*, which means "lodging-places." The Greek word implies "permanent residences."[1]

In my name (14:13-14,26; 15:16; 16:23-24,26). Jesus uses this phrase seven times in this discourse. He is not talking about simply using His name as a formula tacked onto a request. (Recall the significance of "name" from the note on 1:12, page 23.) Rather, He "means that prayer is to be in accordance with all that the name stands for"[2]—prayer must proceed from faith in Christ and be consistent with His character, His priorities, and His mission.

Counselor (14:16,26; 15:26; 16:7). The Greek word *parakletos* is a challenge for translators. It can mean "one called alongside to help" in a legal trial: an advocate, defense attorney, or character witness. It can mean "an intercessor, a mediator, a spokesman." It can mean a "comforter" or one who "bears witness."[3] Attempts at translation include "Counselor" (RSV, NIV), "Comforter" (KJV), "Helper" (NASB), and "Advocate" (NEB). Most commentators prefer to nearly transliterate the word as "Paraclete" because no one translation conveys all the functions that Jesus says this Person has. "The Paraclete is a *witness* in defense of Jesus and a *spokesman* for him in the context of his trial by his enemies; the Paraclete is a *consoler* of the disciples for he takes Jesus' place among them; the Paraclete is a teacher and guide of the disciples and thus their *helper*."[4]

Peace (14:27, 16:33). This is the usual Jewish greeting or farewell, but Jesus is not using it as an ordinary farewell. The peace *the world gives* (14:27) is a mere good wish, a pleasantry like our "Good-bye." But Jesus gives a real, effective, permanent peace independent of outward circumstances. In Hebrew thought, peace is not just the absence of war, but a "positive blessing."[5] Peace is wholeness and well-being in all areas of life—physical, psychological, political, etc.—because of God's presence.[6] Peace is the harmony that begins when people are in right relationship to God, for this and this alone produces justice, righteousness, prosperity, health, and security.[7]

---

2. Read 14:1–16:33 again, and write down everything Jesus says about the following topics:

the Father _____

_____

_____

_____

_____

_____

the Son _____

_____

_____

_____

_____

_____

_____

the Spirit _____

_____

For Thought and Discussion: a. Truth is a primary characteristic of the Father (7:28), the Son (14:6), the Spirit (14:17), and God's worshipers (4:23-24). What does this tell you about God? What does it tell you about you?

b. What might be the connection between worshiping "in spirit and in truth" (4:24) and the work of "the Spirit of truth"?

For Thought and Discussion: Why does it glorify the Father when Jesus grants prayers offered in His name (14:13)?

149

Optional Application: How can you conform your prayers to Jesus' will by abiding in Him and His words?

For Thought and Discussion: a. In 14:1–16:33, what is the relationship between the Father's love and Jesus' obedience? (Compare 10:17-18.)

b. What is the relationship between God's love for us and our obedience?

c. What relationship does Jesus describe between our love for God and our obedience?

d. What is the relationship between belief and obedience?

e. How is abiding or remaining in God related to love and obedience?

f. How is Jesus' obedience (14:32) like what He expects of us? How are His commands to us like and unlike the Father's commands to Him?

prayer _____

_____

_____

_____

_____

_____

the world (its relationship to Jesus, to the Spirit, to the disciples)

_____

_____

_____

_____

_____

peace _____

_____

_____

150

_____

_____

obedience/commands _____

_____

_____

_____

_____

_____

love _____

_____

_____

_____

_____

_____

_____

belief _____

_____

_____

_____

_____

_____

Optional Application: What would it mean for you to love other Christians as Jesus loved His disciples and as He has loved you (13:34, 15:12-13)? Think of some specific acts of love you should be practicing.

Optional Application: How can you obey Jesus by laying down your life for others this week? Pray and be specific about your plans.

Command(ed)(s) . . . commandment(s) (10:18; 12:49-50; 14:15,21,31; 15:10,12,14,17). We may feel that commandments characterize the old covenant rather than the new covenant in Jesus, but Jesus' whole life was focused on the Father's commandments, and Jesus expected His disciples to focus their lives on His com-

For Thought and Discussion: Do you trust the Father and Jesus (14:1)? How do your actions show trust or the lack of it? How can you grow in trust? What past experiences may hinder you from fully trusting God? You might ask other Christians to pray with you about some of these questions.

mandments. Belief in Jesus, love for Jesus, and obedience to Jesus' word(s)/teaching/command(s) are closely intertwined. In this discourse, Jesus summarizes His commands in one command.

Your response

3. On page 30, write what you've learned about Jesus from 14:1-16:33.

4. What one insight from this lesson would you like to take to heart and apply this week?

_____

_____

_____

_____

_____

5. How do you fall short or need to grow in this area? How would you like it to affect what you are and do?

_____

_____

_____

_____

_____

6. What steps can you take toward this end?

_____

_____

_____

_____

_____

7. List any questions you have about this lesson.

_____

_____

_____

For the group

Warm-up. Ask, "If you knew you were going to die tomorrow, what would be your parting words to your closest friends or your children?"

Questions. This lesson is less directive than most. It is a chance for you to make some raw observations and pull them together into principles on various topics. You may prefer to discuss two or three of the topics in depth, rather than trying to cover them all. Let group members list everything they observed on a given topic, then ask them to summarize what the observations reveal. Make connections among the topics, such as, "What does all this tell us about the Trinity?" Or, "How are love and obedience related in Jesus' teaching?" Be sure to allow time to share your plans for application.

Worship. Praise God for the specific truths about each topic you have discussed. Praise the Spirit for who He is and what He does in your lives. Praise Jesus for granting your prayers, giving you peace, showing you what love and obedience are, and promising to abide with and in you. Praise the Father for sending Jesus and the Spirit, and for answering your prayers.

1. Morris, page 638; compare Brown, volume 29A, pages 618-619.
2. Morris, page 646.
3. Brown, volume 29A, pages 1136-1137.
4. Brown, volume 29A, page 1137.
5. Morris, pages 657-658.
6. Hartmut Beck and Colin Brown, "Peace," _The New International Dictionary of New Testament Theology,_ volume 2, pages 776-783.
7. Paul D. Hanson, "War, Peace, and Justice in Early Israel," _Bible Review_ (Washington, D.C.: Biblical Archaeological Society, Fall 1987), page 41.

JOHN 14:1-16:33

Parting Words: 2

In lesson sixteen you studied the nine major topics in Jesus' final discourse. As you look at some other important teachings in this section, keep in mind what you have already learned.

Greater things

1. The disciples are understandably grief-stricken that their Master is leaving them. But what will happen because Jesus is going to the Father?

   14:2-3 _____

   _____

   _____

   14:12 _____

   _____

   _____

   14:13-14 _____

   _____

   _____

   16:5-7 _____

   _____

Optional Application: Are you participating in doing greater things than Jesus did (14:12)? Do you believe that you should be? Make it a persistent prayer for God to do these greater things through you and to help you believe that He wants to do so.

Optional Application: How does knowing that Jesus is *the* truth and life affect your actions and attitudes? How do you need to grow or change in this area?

2. What do you think are the "greater things" the disciples will do (14:12)?

_____

_____

_____

_____

_____

Jesus and the Father

3. What does it mean to say that Jesus is . . .

the way (14:6)? _____

_____

_____

_____

the truth? _____

_____

_____

_____

the life? _____

_____

_____

_____

4. What does Philip's question in 14:8 tell you about him?

_____

_____

_____

_____

The vine

True vine (15:1). The vineyard or vine is a symbol for Israel in the Old Testament. Sometimes the vineyard is fruitful (Isaiah 27:2-6), but usually it is "unproductive or desolate and disappointing"[1] to the Lord (Jeremiah 5:10, 12:10-11). As Jesus is the true bread and light, more nourishing and illuminating than the Law, so He is the true vine.

Remain (15:4-7). The Greek verb *meno* occurs forty times in John's Gospel. It implies permanence: "remain," "abide," "stay," "dwell on," "endure." In a common sense it is used for living somewhere for awhile (1:39, 4:40). But John also uses *meno* to show how what pertains to Jesus is permanent. The Spirit, who inspired the prophets temporarily, remained on Jesus (1:32). The food Jesus gives endures (6:27). The fruit He enables in us lasts (15:16).

    Further, John uses *meno* and another verb (*einai*) "to express the permanency of relationship between Father and Son and between Son and Christian."[2] He talks about how the Father and Son abide in each other and in the believer (6:56; 14:10-11; 15:4-10; 17:21,23). In fact, the unity between Jesus and believers (Him in us and us in Him) is patterned on the unity between the Father and Jesus (each in the other). Love expressed in obedience and sacrifice is the binding force (15:4-17, 17:23).

5. What is God's purpose for you (John 15:2,5-8,16)? (*Optional:* See also Romans 8:29; Galatians 5:22-23; Ephesians 2:10, 5:9.)

_____

_____

_____

_____

_____

_____

For Thought and Discussion: What does it mean to say that Jesus is *in* His Father (14:20)? That believers are *in* Jesus? That Jesus is *in* believers?

For Further Study: Compare Jesus' imagery about the vine to Psalm 80:8-19; Jeremiah 6:9; Ezekiel 15:1-6, 17:1-10, 19:10-14; Hosea 10:1, 14:7.

For Further Study: Compare John 15:1-8 to what Paul says about the Body of Christ in 1 Corinthians 12:12-26. What do the images of the vine and the body tell you about your relationships to Jesus and other Christians? What are the implications for your actions and attitudes?

For Thought and Discussion: What does it mean to "bear fruit" (15:2)?

For Thought and Discussion: In what sense are believers clean (15:3)? In what sense do we need periodic cleansing? (Compare 13:8-10.)

Optional Application: How can you abide more deeply in Jesus and His words this week?

6. How is it possible for you to accomplish this purpose (John 15:1-9)?

_____

_____

_____

_____

7. How can a person "remain" or "abide" in Jesus?

_____

_____

_____

_____

8. Describe one experience you have had of being pruned or cleaned by the Father (15:1-3).

_____

_____

_____

_____

_____

The world

Why . . . ? (14:22). There were two Judases among the apostles (Luke 6:16). Little is known about Judas the son of James. In 14:22, he (and probably the other apostles) assumes that Jesus is talking about showing Himself physically as the glorious Messiah. Judas is still imagining the awesome appearance the Jews expect the Messiah to make when He comes. It makes no sense that the Liberator-King will be seen by only a handful of people; He should appear to the world in all His glory and prove His greatness. (Compare 7:3-4.)

This passage helps us understand why after His resurrection Jesus appeared only to a few hundred people, most of whom had been His followers. Like Judas, we might have expected that Jesus would stride into the Temple and knock on the high priest's door.

For Thought and Discussion: How has Jesus overcome the world (16:33)?

9. Why doesn't Jesus show Himself to the world, either right after His resurrection or now (14:22-24)?

_____

_____

_____

_____

10. Why should Christians expect persecution (15:18–16:4)?

_____

_____

_____

_____

11. Why shouldn't Christians be fearful or anxious at the prospect of persecution when Jesus is absent (14:1-4,18,21,27; 16:20-24,32-33)?

_____

_____

_____

_____

_____

159

For Thought and Discussion: Why did Jesus forewarn His disciples about what was going to happen—His imminent departure and their subsequent persecution (14:29; 16:4,32-33)?

For Thought and Discussion: Explain how the Holy Spirit convicts the world about sin, righteousness, and judgment (16:7-11).

12. Why does Jesus' coming remove all excuses for sin (15:22-24)?

_____

_____

_____

_____

_____

Sin and righteousness and judgment (16:8-11). The world (the people deluded by and enslaved to the world system) totally misunderstands what these three things are. That is why the world decided that Jesus was a sinner, that the Jewish leaders and Roman rulers were righteous, and that Jesus deserved to be judged and executed.[3] John 16:9-11 explains what real sin, righteousness, and judgment are.

We don't understand (16:17-18). This was a recurring theme for the disciples, and indeed for everyone who encountered Jesus. Before the Crucifixion and Resurrection, their bewilderment is understandable.

Your response

13. What one insight from this lesson currently seems most significant to you?

_____

_____

_____

_____

_____

14. How do you want this to affect your actions and attitudes?

160

_____

_____

_____

_____

_____

15. What practical steps can you take to cooperate
with God in bringing this about?

_____

_____

_____

_____

16. List any questions you have about 14:1–16:33.

_____

_____

_____

_____

For the group

Warm-up. Ask, "Do you ever experience hostility or
scorn because of your faith in Jesus?" Let one or
more people give examples.

Worship. Praise Jesus for being the way, the truth,
and the life. Thank Him for preparing a dwelling for
each of you in the Father's house, for enabling you
to do even greater things than He did, and for enabling you to bear fruit. Thank the Father for sending the Holy Spirit and for keeping you safe in the
midst of persecution.

1. Brown, volume 29A, page 669.
2. Brown, volume 29, page 510.
3. Morris, pages 697-698.

JOHN 17:1-26

The Lord's Prayer

To most of us "The Lord's Prayer" is Matthew
6:9-13. But John 17 records what Jesus prayed aloud
to the Father just before allowing Himself to be
arrested. In part, this prayer is unique to the crisis
at hand. Yet Hebrews 7:25 tells us that even in
heaven Jesus "always lives to intercede for" His
people, and John 17 gives us a glimpse of what He
is constantly asking the Father to grant.

Read this chapter aloud slowly with the emotions you think Jesus had as He prayed it. Try to
hear Jesus praying these words.

1. We can break this chapter broadly into three
   parts as Jesus prays for three sets of people.
   Below, write down a) for whom Jesus prays in
   each section, b) what He says is true of those
   people, and c) what He asks the Father to do for
   that person or those people.

   | 17:1-5 |
   | a. |
   | |
   | b. |

c.

17:6-19

a.

b.

c.

17:20-26

a.

b.

c.

2. Is Jesus' request in 17:1-5 selfish? Why or why not?

_____

_____

_____

_____

_____

For Thought and Discussion: a. What does 17:5 affirm about Jesus?
b. What does 17:10 say about Him?

For Thought and Discussion: Why do you think Jesus chose not to pray for "the world" (17:9)?

Granted . . . give . . . given (17:2). This Greek verb for "to give" is used seventy-six times in John's Gospel, seventeen times in chapter 17 alone. It is used most often for the Father giving to the Son, and second for the Son giving to His disciples. "What *'grace'* is in the Pauline Epistles, *'giving'* is in the Fourth Gospel."[1]

3. According to chapter 17 . . .

what has the Father given the Son?

_____

_____

_____

_____

_____

_____

_____

what has the Son given His disciples?

_____

_____

_____

165

For Thought and Discussion: What do the following phrases mean:

"protect them by the power of your name" (17:11);

"so that they may be one as we are one" (17:11);

"they are not of the world" (17:14)?

For Thought and Discussion: Why doesn't Jesus want to take His disciples out of the world since they aren't "of" it (17:14-16)?

Sanctify (17:17-19). To "make holy, separate."[2] That is, separated from the world's outlook and control, and committed to the outlook and control of the Holy Spirit of God.

Know (17:3,25). Jesus sometimes uses this word of knowing facts (17:7-8), but here He has in mind knowledge of a person, an intimate relationship. It is the way wives know their husbands or children know their parents.

4. In 17:3,25-26, what does Jesus say about intimately knowing the Father and the Son?

5. What can you do to come to know the Father more intimately?

6. Why is unity among believers, the Father, and the Son crucial (17:21,23)?

_____

_____

_____

Your response

7. Add any thoughts from chapter 17 to your list on page 30.

8. What one aspect of Jesus' prayer currently seems most significant to you?

_____

_____

_____

_____

_____

9. How would you like this to affect your life in a deeper way?

_____

_____

_____

_____

10. What can you do to let this truth affect your thoughts and actions this week?

_____

_____

_____

_____

11. List any questions you have about 17:1-26.

Optional Application: a. What steps can you take to foster greater unity among the Christians with whom you worship and serve God?
b. How can you grow to know God more intimately and become more one with the Father and the Son?

167

_____

_____

_____

_____

For the group

Warm-up. Ask, "What one thing would you most like Jesus to ask the Father to do for you?"

Worship. Praise Jesus for glorifying the Father in His death, and praise the Father for glorifying Jesus. Thank Jesus for enabling you to know Him and His Father by revelation. Thank God for sanctifying you by the truth of Jesus' words, for giving you the Father's protection, and for making you one with each other and with the Father and the Son.

1. Morris, page 718, note 6, quoting Edwin A. Abbott, _Johannine Grammar_ (London, 1906), page 2742.
2. Morris, page 730

JOHN 18:1-19:16

Condemned

After His prayer, Jesus led His disciples out of Jerusalem, to their camping place on the lower slopes of the Mount of Olives (Luke 21:37, 22:39). It was an olive grove called Gethsemane (Matthew 26:36). John tells us nothing of the anguished prayer Jesus offered to His Father there as He struggled for the last time to choose the destiny the Father willed (Luke 22:40-46). For John that struggle is summed up in 12:27-28, so he skips to the moment when the betrayer arrived. John gives us only glimpses of the next twelve hours' interrogation and torture. Ask God to impress Jesus' character on your heart as you read 18:1-19:16.

Arrest (18:1-12)

> ### Study Skill—Five Ws and an H
> When you study a passage on your own, come to it with as many questions as you can think of. Keep in mind the five Ws and an H: Who, What, When, Where, Why, and How.

1. Use the five Ws and an H to explore 18:1-12. Answer the first four questions, then make up two of your own.

   Who (was there)? _____

   _____

_____

_____

_____

What (happened)? _____

_____

_____

_____

When (did the events take place)? _____

_____

_____

Where (did the events take place)? _____

_____

_____

Why? _____

_____

_____

How? _____

_____

_____

***Soldiers . . . officials from the chief priests and
Pharisees*** (18:3). The Sanhedrin had sent
members of the temple guard, and the Roman
governor had sent a detachment of the Roman
troops stationed in Jerusalem. This rather large
group went to Gethsemane with arms and lan-
terns. Both the Jewish and Roman authorities
evidently expected that the police would have
to flush out a dangerous revolutionary hiding in
the garden, and then perhaps fight a skirmish
with His followers.[1]

Sword (18:10). The Greek word denotes a long dagger, not a full-sized sword. It was not legal to carry weapons during feasts, and a dagger could be concealed.[2] Peter was apparently feeling frightened and revolutionary enough to ignore religious rules.

Cup (18:11). "In the Old Testament the 'cup' often has associations of suffering and of the wrath of God" (Psalm 75:8; Isaiah 51:17,22; Ezekiel 23:31-33).[3] Jesus drank the cup of God's wrathful judgment upon sin on behalf of humanity.

2. Think about what happens to Jesus and how He responds in 18:1-12. What do you learn about His character, His mission, and what He values? What details give you these impressions?

_____

_____

_____

_____

_____

_____

_____

For Thought and Discussion: What does "I am he" (18:5,6,8) imply? (Recall 4:26, 8:58, 13:19.) Why do you think the soldiers fell to the ground at these words (18:6)?

For Thought and Discussion: New Testament writers usually use the phrase "so that the words . . . would be fulfilled" of Old Testament Scripture. What does it say about Jesus that John uses this phrase in 18:9 of the fulfillment of Jesus' words in 6:39 and 17:12?

3. Use your observations about Jesus at His arrest and trials as springboards to praise Him.

Interview with Annas (18:13-27)

None of the four Gospels records all of the interviews and trials that Jesus underwent between perhaps 3 a.m. and noon on Friday:[4]

Jewish trials
1. Interrogation by Annas (John 18:12-14,19-23).
2. Informal trial by the Sanhedrin before dawn (Matthew 26:57-68; Mark 14:53-65; Luke 22:54,63-65; John 18:24).
3. Formal trial after dawn (Matthew 27:1, Mark 15:1, Luke 22:66-71).

171

For Further Study:
Study and compare
the accounts of Jesus'
trials in all four Gos-
pels. What unique
perspectives does
each add?

Roman trials
1. First appearance before Pilate (Matthew 27:2,11-14; Mark 15:1-5; Luke 23:1-5; John 18:28-38).
2. Before Herod Antipas (Luke 23:8-12).
3. Final appearance before Pilate (Matthew 27:15-26, Mark 15:6-15, Luke 23:13-25, John 18:39-19:16a).

Annas (18:13). Although Caiaphas was the ruling high priest, many Jews may still have felt that Annas was the legitimate high priest. "In any case Annas appears to have been a very wily person and one well able to assert himself. Not only was he high priest, but in time five of his sons occupied that office, as did Caiaphas, his son-in-law. . . . He was in all probability the real power in the land, whatever the legal technicalities."[5] Moreover, Annas's family may have been the principle owner of the businesses that Jesus had twice expelled from the Temple.[6]

Another disciple (18:15). This may have been John. His father Zebedee was a prosperous fisherman with employees (Mark 1:20). It was not unusual for Galilean fish merchants to have contracts with large households in Jerusalem, so John may have become *known to the high priest* (the Greek expression implies some intimacy) through such commerce. Or, since there is some evidence that John's was a priestly family, he may have gotten to know the high priest in that way. This is all speculation, however. The disciple named in 18:15 may have been Joseph of Arimathea (19:38), Nicodemus, or someone else.[7]

Questioned (18:19). According to Jewish legal procedure, the accused was held to be innocent and not even on trial until at least two independent witnesses had given testimony that agreed. The accused could not be asked to incriminate himself. Annas was conducting an unofficial interrogation to gather evidence for a trial, but Jesus insisted that Annas should be talking to witnesses, not to the accused (18:19-21).[8]

172

Annas's questions about Jesus' *disciples and his teaching* pointed to both religious and political charges. According to Deuteronomy 13:2-6, 18:20, a false prophet "leads others astray" (His disciples) and "falsely presumes to speak in God's name"[9] (His teaching). At the same time, Annas wanted to know what Jesus taught His disciples in private regarding politics: were they being trained for an uprising or fed subversive ideas? Jesus answered that His private teaching was wholly consistent with His public teaching, so Annas should follow the legal rules and talk to witnesses (18:20-21).

Testify (18:23). Again Jesus pointed out the illegality of this interrogation and demanded justice—in this case, legal evidence. (Remember how John's Gospel stresses witness and testimony.)

Annas sent him . . . to Caiaphas (18:24). Annas realized he was getting nowhere trying to make the prisoner incriminate Himself. John tells us nothing about what happened in the preliminary or official trials before Caiaphas and the Sanhedrin. John's source of information was apparently at Annas's house. The Synoptics state that witnesses were not found to agree on evidence against Jesus, but that the Sanhedrin found Jesus guilty of blasphemy and sent Him to the governor to be tried on political charges.

4. What attitudes (toward self, others, and circumstances) does Jesus show in 18:19-23?

_____

_____

_____

_____

_____

_____

_____

173

For Thought and Discussion: If Jesus had felt hatred toward His captors or the man who struck Him, what could He have done? How was His actual conduct different from what He could have done? Why is this important for us to remember?

For Thought and Discussion: Are you like Peter in any ways? If so, how?

Study Skill—Interpretation
It's crucial to study Scripture in light of Scripture. In particular, passages that seem at first glance to contradict each other actually prove to shed light on each other when examined more closely. Question 5 is an example. It uses John 18:22-23 to illuminate Luke 6:27-31.

5. How is John 18:22-23 consistent with Luke 6:27-31?

_____

_____

_____

_____

_____

6. What do you learn about Peter's character from 13:36-38; 18:10,15-18,25-27?

_____

_____

_____

_____

_____

_____

_____

Trial before Pilate (18:28-19:16)

Early morning (18:28). Jewish law required that trials involving the death sentence could not be held at night, so the Sanhedrin probably held its final trial at daybreak. Jesus was then taken immediately to Pilate. Roman courts normally began work at daybreak, so there was nothing

174

unusual about bringing a prisoner to the governor between 6 and 7 a.m.[10]

Ceremonial uncleanness (18:28). Gentiles were not automatically unclean. However, a family burial place or a woman with a period might defile a Gentile's home. The defilement from entering such a home lasted for seven days (Numbers 19:11-14), so the Jewish leaders would have missed the entire festival.[11]

Pilate (18:29). Pontius Pilate was prefect of Judea from 26 to 36 AD. His Jewish subjects detested him; Philo and Josephus accused him of robbery, murder, atrocities, and social blunders (compare Luke 13:1). He had provoked a riot by parading his soldiers with a portrait of the emperor on a Jewish holy day, for the Jews considered the portrait an idol. Pilate was disciplined for that, and he knew Rome would punish him if there were riots over a controversy about a supposed Messiah.[12]

A criminal (18:30). Since Pilate had to have authorized the Roman soldiers at Jesus' arrest, he must have known the Jews were accusing Jesus of political crimes. However, he followed proper procedure by asking for a formal charge (18:29). This put the Jews in an awkward position. They knew they "had no charge that would stand up in a Roman court of law,"[13] so they made the vague charge that he was a doer of evil. Naturally, Pilate could not accept this.

No right to execute (18:31). Unless a person broke a Roman law, the Romans preferred to let conquered peoples apply their own laws. However, the Roman governors rarely allowed local courts to pass death sentences. Especially in a volatile province like Judea, local judges might start executing Roman sympathizers on pretexts. Furthermore, the Sanhedrin did not want Jesus stoned as a false prophet; they wanted Him crucified as a political criminal. The Jews equated crucifixion with hanging, and "anyone who is hung on a tree is under God's curse" (Deuteronomy 21:23). Stoning might make Jesus appear to be a martyred prophet, but hanging/crucifixion would prove that God had rejected Him.[14]

For Further Study:
Jesus knew that it was necessary for Him to die by crucifixion, not stoning (3:14, 8:28, 12:32-34). Why was it necessary for Him to die on a cross? See Galatians 3:23.

175

Optional Application: a. What implications does the statement, "My kingdom is not of this world" (18:36) have for your priorities and actions?

b. What implications does the statement, "Everyone on the side of truth listens to me" (18:37) have for you?

For Thought and Discussion: What impressions do you get of the chief priests' priorities from 18:28,38-40; 19:6-7,15,21,31? Which parts of God's Law were most important to them, and which parts were less important?

Is that your own idea (18:34). "If Pilate asked it of himself, the question would have meant, 'Art thou a political King, conspiring against Caesar'! If he had asked it of Caiaphas' prompting, it would have meant, 'Art Thou the Messianic King of Israel?' The answer to the first question would have been, 'No.' The answer to the second question, 'Yes.'"[15]

You are right in saying I am a king (18:37). More literally, "You say I am a king." Jesus could not deny that He was a king, but this was not the title He would choose in explaining Himself to a man with Roman notions of kingship.[16] NEB reads, "'King' is your word."

Barabbas (18:40). Ironically, this man in whose place Jesus died really was a violent revolutionary, probably a leader (Matthew 27:16, Mark 15:7, Luke 23:18-19). He was apparently a part of the resistance movement and a hero to the Jews. Also ironically, his name means "son of Abba" or "son of the father."

Flogged (19:1). The Gospels are extremely reserved in describing Jesus' sufferings. They hardly play on the readers emotions at all. "Scourging was a brutal affair. It was inflicted by a whip of several thongs, each of which was loaded with pieces of bone or metal. It could make pulp of a man's back."[17]

No friend of Caesar (19:12). The Sanhedrin threatened Pilate that if he failed to do their will, they would accuse him of incompetence in handling traitors. If Pilate had been a model governor, he would not have been worried, but "Pilate's record was not one to be subjected to close scrutiny."[18]

7. Of what crimes was Jesus accused (18:30,33; 19:7,19)?

_____

_____

_____

176

8. What evidence was there for or against these accusations (8:58, 10:30, 18:36-38)?

_____

_____

_____

_____

_____

9. Explain in your own words what Jesus says about . . .

His Kingdom (18:33-36) _____

_____

_____

_____

_____

_____

His mission (18:37) _____

_____

_____

_____

_____

power (19:10-11) _____

_____

_____

_____

_____

10. What impressions do you get of Jesus from His behavior in 18:28-19:16?

_____

For Thought and Discussion: Jesus offered no defense in any of His trials. Why do you think He didn't?

For Thought and Discussion: Why do you suppose John stresses that Pilate found Jesus innocent (18:38; 19:4,6)?

For Thought and Discussion: Why do you think Jesus refused to answer Pilate's question in 19:9, although He replied to all the rest?

177

11. What do Pilate's words and actions tell you about his beliefs and character?

_____

_____

_____

_____

_____

Your response

12. Meditate on 18:1-19:16 for awhile. Let the scenes sink in. What aspects seem most personally significant to you?

_____

_____

_____

_____

_____

13. How would you like one of those truths to affect your life more deeply?

_____

_____

_____

_____

14. What practical steps can you take this week to allow this to happen increasingly?

_____

_____

_____

_____

_____

15. List any questions you have about 18:1–19:16.

_____

_____

_____

_____

For the group

Warm-up. Ask, "How would you feel if you were arrested and accused of being a political criminal? What would you do?" This question may help group members put themselves in Jesus' place and see how amazing His behavior was.

Read aloud. Try assigning the various roles in this drama (including the narrator) to different group members. Let the whole group read the lines of the Jews. The main goal of this lesson is to help you see and feel each scene, and especially to let you see Jesus in these events. Imagine yourselves as the crowd shouting "Crucify!" (Have you ever been like this?), then as Jesus looking His interrogators calmly in the eye (Are you enough like Jesus yet to handle such a situation in this way?).

Worship. Praise Jesus for the way He handled His arrest and trials. Praise Him for deliberately accepting the injustice and abuse even though, as God, He had the power to retaliate. Thank Him for the love that moved Him to go through this suffering.

1. F. F. Bruce, _New Testament History_ (Garden City, New York: Doubleday and Company, 1980), pages 195-196.

2. Morris, page 745, note 15.
3. Morris, page 746.
4. Adapted from Irving Jensen, *John: A Self-study Guide* (Chicago: Moody Press, 1970), page 92.
5. Morris, page 749.
6. William Barclay, *The Gospel of John*, volume 2 (Philadelphia: Westminster Press, 1956), page 61.
7. Morris, page 752; Brown, volume 29A, pages 822-823.
8. Barclay, page 58; Morris, page 755.
9. Brown, volume 29A, page 835.
10. Morris, page 762; Brown, volume 29A, page 844.
11. Brown, volume 29A, pages 845-846; Morris, page 763, note 59.
12. J. I. Packer, Merrill C. Tenney, and William White, Jr., *The World of the New Testament* (Nashville, Tennessee: Thomas Nelson Publishers, 1972), page 82; Brown, volume 29A, pages 846-847.
13. Morris, page 764.
14. Brown, volume 29A, pages 849-851; Morris, pages 765-766.
15. Morris, page 768-769, quoting G. Venn Pilcher, *The Gospel according to St. John* (Sydney, Australia, n. d.).
16. Morris, page 770; Brown, volume 29A, pages 853-854.
17. Morris, page 790.
18. Morris, pages 798-799.

JOHN 19:17-42

Crucified

It is noon on Friday. Since last night, Jesus has been betrayed, bound, interrogated, slapped, mocked, tried, scourged within an inch of His life, and finally condemned to death. Read the next stage of the drama in 19:17-42.

Crucified (19:18). "John describes the horror that was crucifixion in a single word." He doesn't play on our emotions.

The Cross may have been shaped like an I, a T, a Y, or like the traditional one. "The victim was fastened to the cross either with cords or nails. The cross beam was fixed so that the victim's feet were off the ground, but not necessarily very high off the ground. There was a horn-like projection (the *sedile*), which the crucified man straddled. This took some of the weight of the body and prevented the flesh tearing from the nails. It was a frightful death."[1] It usually took hours for the blood loss from scourging, exposure to the sun, and restricted circulation and breathing to produce heart failure.

Crucifixion was reserved for the basest criminals and slaves. Roman citizens were not crucified, for even Gentiles regarded this form of execution as an unspeakable disgrace.[2]

His mother's sister (19:25). Comparison of the four Gospels suggests that this was Salome (Mark

181

For Further Study:
Compare John 19:17
to Luke 9:23, 14:27.
What does Jesus'
instruction mean?

15:40) who was John's mother (Matthew 27:56).
John omitted her name as he omitted his own
and his brother's names.[3] If this is correct, then
John was Jesus' cousin. Since Jesus' own brothers did not believe in Him, it was natural for
Him to commit His mother into the care of a
near relative who was also a close friend
(19:27).

Wine vinegar (19:29). "A cheap wine, the kind of
drink that was used by the masses." It was
drunk "well diluted with water."[4] Along with a
sponge and some *hyssop* (a plant with long
branches), the wine was apparently provided for
the victims.

It is finished (19:30). The Synoptics record that
after drinking, Jesus uttered a loud cry just
before His death (Matthew 27:50). In Greek it is
one word: *Tetelestai!* Ancient invoices have
been unearthed in Egypt with this word written
across them; the commercial meaning may have
been something like "Paid in Full." Jesus had
brought His great work of redemption to com-
pletion and fulfillment.

Gave up his spirit (19:30). This was not a usual way
in which Greeks or Jews described death. There
was something uncommonly peaceful and
voluntary about Jesus' death.[5]

Did not want the bodies left (19:31). Jewish law
forbade leaving the body of an executed criminal "on the tree overnight" (Deuteronomy
21:23). The corpse had to be buried before
sunset, lest the Jews "desecrate the land the
LORD your God is giving you as an inheritance."
This was especially important because that Friday was not just *the day of Preparation* for a
Sabbath, but for *a special Sabbath*—the beginning of Passover. The Romans customarily left
the bodies of criminals on their crosses as warnings to others, so the Jewish leaders had to get
Pilate's permission to have the bodies taken
down.

Legs broken (19:31). A crucified person could pro-
long his life by taking some of his body's weight
on his feet. When his legs were broken, his

chest was more fully constricted, and he quickly died from lack of blood and air flow.[6]

---

1. John has carefully chosen what he says about Jesus' crucifixion. The account is brief. Much of what we read here is unique to this Gospel, and John omits much of what the Synoptics tell us. Hence, it is reasonable to assume that everything John records is significant.

How is it significant that . . .

Pilate worded the charge against Jesus as he did and posted it in all three of the major languages of Palestine (19:19-22)?

_____

_____

_____

_____

_____

the soldiers cast lots for Jesus' clothes (19:23-24)?

_____

_____

_____

_____

_____

Jesus gave His mother into John's care (19:25-27)?

_____

_____

_____

_____

_____

For Thought and Discussion: Until Jesus' arrest, John barely mentions the words *king* and *kingdom* (1:49, 3:3-5, 6:15, 12:13-15), but they are prominent in 18:28-19:22. Why do you think John emphasizes Jesus' kingship in the trial and crucifixion but not in the earlier ministry? What does the Gospel as a whole reveal about Jewish ideas of the Messiah's kingship, and about Jesus' view of His kingship?

For Thought and Discussion: John is fond of irony, in which things people say and do with one intended meaning have a deeper meaning unknown to them. What irony do you find in the following?

"I find no basis for a charge against him" (18:38).

"Here is the man!" (19:5).

"We have no king but Caesar" (19:15).

The charge, "Jesus of Nazareth, the King of the Jews" (19:19-21).

The Jews did not want their land defiled by Jesus' body on a cross overnight (19:31).

Jesus said He was thirsty (John 19:28; compare Psalm 22:15, 69:21)?

_____

_____

_____

_____

Jesus said, "It is finished" (John 19:30; compare John 1:29; Hebrews 9:11-15,24-28; 10:11-14)?

_____

_____

_____

_____

_____

_____

Jesus' legs were not broken, but His side was pierced (John 19:31-37)?

_____

_____

_____

_____

_____

2. How is it personally important to you that . . .

Jesus was convicted of being the King of the Jews?

_____

_____

_____

_____

_____

Jesus said, "It is finished" when He died?

_____

_____

_____

_____

_____

3. Why is important that Jesus' death fulfilled so
many Old Testament prophecies?

_____

_____

_____

_____

_____

**For Thought and
Discussion:** John
says nothing about
how horrible scourg-
ing and crucifixion
were. Why do you
think he so under-
states Jesus' suffer-
ings? Why doesn't he
emphasize the physi-
cal agony?

**For Thought and
Discussion:** What
does 19:26-27 tell
you about Jesus'
character? How could
He think about His
mother at a time like
this?

Joseph (19:38). He was rich (Matthew 27:57), a
member of the Sanhedrin (Luke 23:50-51), and
a secret disciple of Jesus who had not taken part
in condemning Him. As one of the Jewish leaders, it would have been extremely hard for
Joseph to follow Jesus openly (John 7:48-52,
12:42).

Myrrh and aloes (19:39). "It was the custom to put
spices of this kind in with the sheets round the
body."[7] Myrrh "is a fragrant resin" from a tree,
"used by the Egyptians in embalming." Aloes
"is a powdered aromatic sandalwood used for
perfuming bedding or clothes, but not normally
for burial. . . . The purpose of the aloes was
probably to counteract unpleasant odor and
slow down corruption."[8] (The modern aloe vera
gel comes from a quite different plant.)
    Seventy-five pounds of spices was a huge
and expensive amount; such a large quantity
was normally used only for royal burials.[9]

A new tomb (19:41). "Tombs were commonly hewn out of the solid rock, and closed with heavy stones. The stone at the mouth would run in a groove and finish right over the opening. Such tombs were expensive, and there would be a tendency to use them again and again."[10]

4. What were Joseph and Nicodemus risking by asking for Jesus' body and burying it?

_____

_____

_____

_____

_____

5. How is it significant that these two did this while the apostles had all fled (Mark 14:50)?

_____

_____

_____

_____

_____

6. Jesus said that His crucifixion would glorify Him and the Father (12:23, 17:1). How did such an awful experience glorify Them?

_____

_____

_____

_____

_____

_____

Your response

7. Take some time to meditate on Jesus' death. What strikes you as important? How has this death affected your life? What difference would you like it to make to your life?

_____

_____

_____

_____

_____

_____

8. What can you do this week to let these events soak into your heart and begin to affect you?

_____

_____

_____

_____

9. List any questions you have about 19:17-42.

_____

_____

_____

_____

For the group

Warm-up. Ask several people to describe the worst thing they have ever suffered for someone else.

Worship. Praise Jesus for finishing His agonizing work just as the Father had willed it. Praise God for having all of these events under control.

1. Morris, page 805. Morris also quotes a graphic description of the torture of being crucified.
2. E. Brandenburger, "Cross," *New International Dictionary of New Testament Theology*, volume 1, pages 392-393.
3. Morris, page 811.
4. Morris, page 813.
5. Morris, pages 815-816.
6. Morris, pages 817-818.
7. Morris, page 825.
8. Brown, volume 29A, page 940.
9. Morris, page 825.
10. Morris, page 826.

JOHN 20:1-31

Resurrection

By dusk on Friday, Joseph and Nicodemus had finished burying the dead body of Jesus. The disciples were in hiding, fearing their own arrest, torture, and death. All their dreams of national liberation and spiritual revival had died when their Master had aptly cried "It is finished." While every other Jew in Jerusalem was celebrating the Passover, commemorating freedom from Egyptian slavery, the disciples of Jesus were cowering in fear. As the whole city was enjoying rest on the Sabbath, the disciples sat numb with grief.

Saturday passed. Night fell again. Shortly before dawn on Sunday, the women disciples who had followed Jesus from Galilee gathered to finish the burial Joseph and Nicodemus had begun (Matthew 28:1; Mark 16:1; Luke 23:55-24:1,10). As you read John 20:1-31, try to sense what Jesus' friends may have felt in these episodes.

The stone had been removed (20:1). The Greek
　　implies that it was not rolled away, but lifted up
　　out of its groove in some violent way.[1]

Folded up (20:7). "In recent years this has often
　　been taken to mean that the grave clothes were
　　just as they had been when placed round the
　　body. That is to say, Jesus' body rose through
　　the grave-clothes without disturbing them. This
　　is not inconsistent with the language, but it

should be borne in mind that John does not say this. That the headcloth was not with the others scarcely supports this, for had this been the case it would have been right alongside them, with no more than the length of the neck (if that) between them. . . . However, whatever be the truth of this, John is plainly describing an orderly scene, not one of wild confusion. This means that the body had not been taken by grave-robbers. They would never have left the cloths wrapped neatly. They would have taken the body, cloths and all, or would have torn the cloths off and scattered them."[2] The early Church bishop John Chrysostom commented that myrrh "glues linen to the body not less firmly than lead."[3]

---

1. What evidence of Jesus' resurrection is recorded in 20:1-21:14?

2. The disciples still did not understand that the Scriptures predicted the Resurrection even after they observed evidence that began to convince them that a resurrection had occurred (20:9). Why is this significant?

3. What do these passages suggest about the resurrected Jesus, especially about His body?

20:14, 21:4 _____

_____

_____

20:19,26 _____

_____

_____

20:20,27 _____

_____

_____

4. Put yourself in Mary's place in 20:10-18, and read the passage meditatively a few times. How would she feel . . .

alone at the empty tomb (20:10-15)?

_____

_____

_____

when Jesus says her name (20:16)?

_____

_____

_____

5. Why do you think Mary recognized Jesus when He said her name (20:16)? (See 10:3-4.)

_____

_____

_____

_____

_____

**Optional
Application:** Does
Jesus call you by
name (20:16)? Why
is this important to
you? How does it
affect the way you
feel about and deal
with your
circumstances?

Do not hold on to me (20:17). The Greek means
"Stop clinging to Me."[4] Mary was apparently
holding Jesus in joy and worship, but He
assured her that He had *not yet returned to the
Father*—He would be around for awhile and
there was no need to cling to Him as though He
might vanish. Also, Mary was acting as though
everything was the same between them, but in
fact the Resurrection had changed many things.

6. What is significant about the way Jesus refers to
God in 20:17?

_____

_____

_____

_____

_____

Peace be with you (20:19,21,26). This is the usual
Jewish greeting, but it is more than just a con-
ventional "Hello" in 20:19. "After their conduct
on Good Friday the disciples might have
expected rebuke or blame. Instead Jesus pro-
nounces peace upon them."[5] He repeats the
blessing of peace when He commissions them
(20:21), perhaps to stress that the promise made
before His arrest (14:27) is being fulfilled as a
result of His death and resurrection.

7. "As the Father has sent me, I am sending you"
(20:21). What does this comparison tell you
about the mission Jesus has given to His
followers?

_____

_____

_____

192

Breathed on them (20:22). Jesus re-created His disciples just as God created man in the beginning (Genesis 2:7). The spirit/breath in a person gives him or her physical life; the Spirit/breath of God gives him or her eternal life. Ezekiel 37:3-5 prophesied this life-giving breathing.

If you forgive . . . (20:23). This verse has led to much disagreement among Christians. What is the meaning of this power to forgive and retain sins? Who has it? How is it exercised? Some interpretations are:

1. Each individual Christian has the authority to pronounce forgiveness upon a believer who confesses a sin.

2. Only ordained priests have the authority to do this, and they do it in the Sacrament of Penance (Confession, Reconciliation).

3. The Church as a whole has the right to forgive or retain a person's sins by admitting or barring him from baptism (by baptizing him, the Church recognizes that the person has become a believer). Or, the Church forgives or retains by recognizing or not recognizing someone as a real believer in some other way.

4. The Church (or an individual Christian?) forgives or retains sins by preaching the gospel. In doing this, the Church (or individual) forgives sins when the hearer repents and believes, and retains sins when the hearer rejects Jesus.

5. The Church (and individual Christians?) "has the power to isolate, repel, and negate evil and sin. . . . It is an effective, not merely a declaratory, power against sin, a power that touches new and old followers of Christ, a power that challenges those who refuse to believe. John does not tell us how or by whom this power was exercised in the community for whom he wrote. . . . Perhaps John's failure to specify may serve as a Christian guideline: . . . one cannot call upon this text as proof that the

193

way in which a particular community exercises this power is not true to Scripture."[6]

There is agreement among Christians that whatever the power to forgive is, and whoever has it, it is not an arbitrary right. "It is the result of the indwelling Spirit and takes place only as that Spirit directs."[7] Only those who are listening to the Spirit have the right to exercise this authority.

---

8. a. Think about the authority Jesus' gives His disciples in 20:23. What do you think He is authorizing them to do?

_____

_____

_____

_____

_____

  b. How is this relevant to you?

_____

_____

_____

_____

_____

9. What did Thomas realize when he saw Jesus (20:28)? Explain in your own words.

_____

_____

_____

_____

10. What can we learn from Thomas's experience (20:24-29)?

_____
_____
_____
_____
_____

For Thought and Discussion: a. In your view, is Thomas's response to the news of resurrection unreasonable (20:24-25)? Why or why not?

b. As it turned out, did Thomas have to put his finger in Jesus' wounds in order to believe (20:27-29)? Why is this important?

Many other miraculous signs (20:30). John explains that he has selected a few episodes of Jesus' life and omitted a great deal. We should never imagine that the Gospels tell us everything Jesus said and did, only everything we need to know for faith and life. They are not the biographies of a dead prophet, but a selective introduction to a living Person.[8]

The "signs" include the works Jesus did in chapters 2 through 12, but in chapter 20 John is probably thinking above all of the Resurrection.

11. Three verbs for "to see" occur especially frequently in chapter 20. Why do you suppose John emphasizes seeing in this chapter? (What does seeing have to do with the point of the chapter?)

_____
_____
_____
_____
_____

Your response

12. What one truth in these resurrection appearances stands out as personally significant to you?

_____

195

_____

_____

_____

13. How have you seen this truth affecting your life already?

_____

_____

_____

_____

14. How would you like it to affect what you do and think more than it does now?

_____

_____

_____

_____

15. What steps can you take to cooperate with God in making this possible?

_____

_____

_____

_____

16. List any questions you have about 20:1-31.

_____

_____

For the group

Warm-up. Ask several people to tell briefly what convinces them that Jesus was really raised from the dead.

Worship. Praise the resurrected Lord, whose body was so changed that He could pass through walls, but who continues to bear the marks of His suffering. Thank Him for what His resurrection has accomplished for you.

1. Morris, page 831.
2. Morris, page 833.
3. Morris, page 833, note 16.
4. Morris, page 840.
5. Morris, page 844.
6. Brown, volume 29A, pages 1044-1045. Morris, pages 847-850, explains why he supports view 4.
7. Morris, page 848.
8. Morris, page 855, note 80.

JOHN 21:1-25 AND REVIEW

Epilogue

Jesus appeared off and on to His disciples for forty days after the Resurrection (Acts 1:3). John chose to record only one more of those appearances (20:30, 21:25) to make several important points in closing his Gospel. Read 21:1-25.

At the seashore (21:1-25)

1. What do you think is the central point John means to make by including this episode?

_____

_____

_____

_____

That night (21:3). It is still the custom of commercial fishermen on the Sea of Galilee to fish after sunset and before sunrise.[1]

_____

2. a. Jesus' appearance was quite changed (21:4,12). How did the disciples come to recognize Him on this occasion (21:6-7)?

_____

For Further Study: Compare John's and Peter's personalities (13:6-9,22-26,36-38; 18:10,15-18,25-27; 19:25-27; 20:3-8; 21:7-8,15-23).

For Thought and Discussion: Why do you think the disciples did not *dare* to ask Jesus who He was (21:12)?

199

For Thought and Discussion: What do you think Jesus meant by "Do you truly love me *more than these*" (21:15)? More than who or what?

For Thought and Discussion: Why do you suppose Peter kept answering "You know that . . ." (21:15-18)?

_____

_____

b. What do you think is the signficance of this?

_____

_____

_____

_____

_____

3. What did the disciples learn about Jesus from this appearance (21:12-13)? (*Optional:* Compare Luke 24:41-43.)

_____

_____

_____

_____

_____

Love (21:15-17). Peter uses *phileo* all three times, but Jesus uses *agapao* the first two times and *phileo* the third. Many interpreters see significance in this change. Some of them regard *agapao* as a higher, more profound love than *phileo*. Others think *agapao* is cooler and more intellectual than warm *phileo*. Unfortunately, these two views contradict each other. But John tends to use *phileo* and *agapao* almost interchangeably (see page 53), so there may be no significance in the shift of words. Also, Jesus and Peter were probably speaking Aramaic, which does not have two slightly distinct words for love.[2]

4. In the presence of Peter's colleagues, Jesus three times asked Peter if he loved Him. Why do you think He did this?

200

_____

_____

_____

_____

_____

5. Explain in your own words the three-fold commission Jesus gave Peter in response to his three-fold declaration of love.

_____

_____

_____

_____

_____

6. Why was love for Jesus an essential requirement for this job?

_____

_____

_____

_____

_____

_____

7. Explain in your own words the related essential qualification for Peter's job (21:19,22).

_____

_____

_____

_____

_____

_____

For Thought and Discussion: What would you say if Jesus, knowing all you have done this week, asked you, "Do you love Me?" How would you feel?

Optional Application: How are Jesus' instructions to you like and unlike those He gave Peter? How well are you fulfilling your instructions? How could you improve?

For Thought and Discussion: How does John compare himself to Peter in 21:19,22 and 21:20?

201

Stretch out your hands (21:18). Possibly a prophecy that Peter would be crucified, as in fact he was in the 60s AD.

Your response

8. What one insight from chapter 21 seems personally significant to you?

_____

_____

_____

_____

_____

9. How would you like it to affect your life more than it already is?

_____

_____

_____

_____

_____

10. What can you do this week toward this growth?

_____

_____

_____

_____

_____

11. List any questions you have about 21:1-25.

_____

_____

Review

If much of what you have studied seems vague or
fragmented, a review can help you tie the book
together. It is also helpful to review how your efforts
to apply what you've learned have actually affected
you. If you have extra time after studying chapter
21, you can begin your review of the book. However, a thorough review will probably take you several hours of preparation (and discussion, if you are
meeting with a group).

The best beginning for a review is to reread the
entire Gospel and glance through the lessons. If this
sounds like more time than you can afford, a half-
hour of reviewing the previous lessons and thumb-
ing through the book should bring back the most
important things you have learned. Look particu-
larly at what you noticed in the overview.

As you review the Gospel, jot answers to questions 12 through 20. Some relevant verses are suggested for some questions, but don't feel you must
look at all of these or only these. Also, don't force
yourself to answer all parts of every question; go
into as much depth as you can. Finally, don't treat
the questions as a comprehensive final exam.
Instead, imagine yourself explaining these things to
a nonChristian. Your goals are to understand John's
Gospel well enough to let it influence your life and
to explain the gospel to ordinary people.

12. John 20:31 is the Evangelist's statement of his
    purpose. What do the following terms mean?

    to believe (in Jesus, or that Jesus is the Christ)

    _____

    _____

    _____

    _____

    _____

Jesus is the Christ _____

_____

_____

_____

_____

Jesus is the Son of God _____

_____

_____

_____

_____

by believing you may have life in His name

_____

_____

_____

_____

_____

13. What evidence does John's Gospel give that Jesus is the Christ and the Son of God?

_____

_____

_____

_____

_____

_____

14. Jesus says over and over "I am." What does it mean that Jesus is . . .

the true bread, the bread of life (6:1-59)?

_____

_____

_____

_____

the true light, the light of the world (1:9,
3:19-21, 8:12, 9:1-41)?

_____

_____

_____

_____

the gate (10:7,9) and the way (14:6)? _____

_____

_____

_____

the good shepherd (10:11,14)? _____

_____

_____

_____

the resurrection and the life (11:25, 14:6)?

_____

_____

_____

_____

_____

the true vine (15:1,5)? _____

_____

_____

_____

_____

the truth (14:6)? _____

_____

_____

_____

_____

15. (*Optional*) What did Jesus reveal about Himself and His mission through each of the signs John recorded?

changing water into wine
clearing the vendors from the Temple
healing the official's son
healing the paralytic at the pool on the Sabbath
feeding the five thousand
walking on the water
healing the blind man
raising Lazarus
being crucified and resurrected

16. What does "living water" mean, and why is it important (4:10-14, 7:37-39, 14:26-27, 15:26, 16:7-11, 20:21-23)?

_____

_____

_____

_____

_____

_____

17. Summarize the mission—the "work"—for which the Father sent Jesus into the world (1:12-14,18; 3:16-17; 4:34; 5:24-30; 10:17-18; 12:23-24,27-28,46; 18:37; 19:30).

_____

_____

_____

_____

_____

_____

18. Describe the response Jesus wants His disciples to make to His identity and mission (3:18-21; 6:35,40,53-54; 7:37; 8:31,51; 10:27; 12:24-26; 13:13-17; 15:7-14; 17:22-23; 20:15-23).

_____

_____

_____

_____

_____

_____

19. Have you noticed any areas (thoughts, attitudes, opinions, behavior) in which you have changed as a result of your study of John's Gospel? If so, what are they?

_____

_____

_____

_____

_____

20. Look back over the entire study at questions in which you expressed a desire to make some application. Are you satisfied with your follow-through? Ask God to show you any areas in which you should continue to pursue growth. Write anything you decide here.

_____

_____

_____

_____

_____

_____

_____

For the group

Warm-up. Ask the group to think about this question: "How would you respond if Jesus, knowing everything you have done this week, asked you, 'Do you love Me?' How would you feel?" Let anyone answer who wants to.

At the seashore. Don't spend a long time discussing whether the change from *agapao* to *phileo* is significant. Focus on why Jesus asked His question three times, what He was commanding Peter to do, and how all of this is relevant to each of you.

Review. You will probably need at least one full meeting to discuss this review. However, don't try to cover all the questions. Choose a few to delve into deeply. Make sure to allow time for questions 18 through 20, which give you a chance to assess how your efforts at application have gone. This should not be a time of boasting or self-condemnation, but one of mutual encouragement. Look for ways to help each other learn to apply the Scriptures better in the future. Point out the areas in which you see growth in one another. Remind the group that God is responsible for results in changing your lives; you are responsible to keep "abiding" in Him through prayer and obedience.

Ask if anyone still has questions about the Gospel. If there are any questions, let the group try to answer them before you suggest answers yourself. (It is a good idea to let the group do as much for itself as possible, so that everyone will be urged toward maturity.) If you aren't sure about the answers, the sources on pages 211-215 may help.

Evaluation. Plan some time (part or all of a meeting) to evaluate how well your group functioned during your study of John. Some questions you might ask are:

> What did you learn about small group study?
> How well did your study help you grasp the book of John?
> What were the most important truths you discovered together about God?
> What did you like best about your meetings?
> What did you like least? What would you change?
> How well did you meet the goals you set at your first meeting?
> What are group members' current needs? What will you do next?

Worship. Praise Jesus for giving Peter a chance to reaffirm his love and commitment. Thank Him that even your worst failures do not make Him give up on using you for His work. Thank Him also for revealing Himself to you through John's Gospel, and for giving you a group with whom to study it.

1. Morris, page 862, note 9.
2. Morris, pages 871-873; Brown, volume 29, pages 497-499; Brown, volume 29A, pages 1102-1103.

STUDY AIDS

For further information on the material covered in this study, consider the following sources. If your local bookstore does not have them, you can ask the bookstore to order them from the publishers, or find them in a public, university, or seminary library.

Commentaries on John

Brown, Raymond E. *The Gospel According to John*, The Anchor Bible, volumes 29 and 29A (Doubleday, 1966, 1970).
Brown is considered the foremost Johannine scholar of our day, so anyone interested in serious study of historical background, Greek words, and critical scholarship should definitely consult him. However, the ordinary conservative evangelical may find it frustrating to wade through critical comments (such as how various editors composed and revised each passage) to find the material he wants. Brown is not an extreme skeptic regarding the authority of Scripture, and much of his theological commentary is valuable, but he is no conservative.

Morris, Leon. *The Gospel According to John*, The New International Commentary on the New Testament (Eerdmans, 1971).
Leon Morris is both a fine scholar and an evangelical. His book is very readable, and the ordinary student can probably find as much commentary as he needs in it, even if he sometimes disagrees with Morris.

Historical and Background Sources

Bruce, F. F. *New Testament History* (Doubleday, 1980).
A readable history of Herodian kings, Roman governors, philosopn-

ical schools, Jewish sects, Jesus, the early Jerusalem church, Paul, and early gentile Christianity. Well-documented with footnotes for the serious student, but the notes do not intrude.

Harrison, E. F. *Introduction to the New Testament* (Eerdmans, 1971).
   History from Alexander the Great—who made Greek culture dominant in the biblical world—through philosophies, pagan and Jewish religions, Jesus' ministry and teaching (the weakest section), and the spread of Christianity. Very good maps and photographs of the land, art, and architecture of New Testament times.

Packer, James I., Merrill C. Tenney, William White, Jr. *The Bible Almanac* (Thomas Nelson, 1980).
   One of the most accessible handbooks of the people of the Bible and how they lived. Lots of photos and illustrations liven an already readable text.

Concordances, Dictionaries, and Handbooks

A *concordance* lists words of the Bible alphabetically along with each verse in which the word appears. It lets you do your own word studies. An *exhaustive* concordance lists every word used in a given translation, while an *abridged* or *complete* concordance omits either some words, some occurrences of the word, or both.
   The two best exhaustive concordances are *Strong's Exhaustive Concordance* and *Young's Analytical Concordance to the Bible*. Both are available based on the King James Version of the Bible and the New American Standard Bible. *Strong's* has an index by which you can find out which Greek or Hebrew word is used in a given English verse. *Young's* breaks up each English word it translates. However, neither concordance requires knowledge of the original language.
   Among other good, less expensive concordances, *Cruden's Complete Concordance* is keyed to the King James and Revised Versions, and *The NIV Complete Concordance* is keyed to the New International Version. These include all references to every word included, but they omit "minor" words. They also lack indexes to the original languages.

A *Bible dictionary* or *Bible encyclopedia* alphabetically lists articles about people, places, doctrines, important words, customs, and geography of the Bible.
   The New Bible Dictionary, edited by J. D. Douglas, F. F. Bruce, J. I. Packer, N. Hillyer, D. Guthrie, A. R. Millard, and D. J. Wiseman (Tyndale, 1982) is more comprehensive than most dictionaries. Its 1300 pages include quantities of information along with excellent maps, charts, diagrams, and an index for cross-referencing.
   Unger's Bible Dictionary by Merrill F. Unger (Moody, 1979) is equally good and is available in an inexpensive paperback edition.

The *Zondervan Pictorial Encyclopedia* edited by Merrill C. Tenney (Zondervan, 1975, 1976) is excellent and exhaustive, and is being revised and updated in the 1980s. However, its five 1000-page volumes are a financial investment, so all but very serious students may prefer to use it at a church, public, college, or seminary library.

Unlike a Bible dictionary in the above sense, *Vine's Expository Dictionary of New Testament Words* by W. E. Vine (various publishers) alphabetically lists major words used in the King James Version and defines each New Testament Greek word that KJV translates with that English word. *Vine's* lists verse references where that Greek word appears, so that you can do your own cross-references and word studies without knowing any Greek.

Vine's is a good basic book for beginners, but it is much less complete than other Greek helps for English speakers. More serious students might prefer *The New International Dictionary of New Testament Theology*, edited by Colin Brown (Zondervan) or *The Theological Dictionary of the New Testament* by Gerhard Kittel and Gerhard Friedrich, abridged in one volume by Geoffrey W. Bromiley (Eerdmans).

A ***Bible atlas*** can be a great aid to understanding what is going on in a book of the Bible and how geography affected events. Here are a few good choices:

The Macmillan Atlas by Yohanan Aharoni and Michael Avi-Yonah (Macmillan, 1968, 1977) contains 264 maps, 89 photos, and 12 graphics. The many maps of individual events portray battles, movements of people, and changing boundaries in detail.

The New Bible Atlas by J. J. Bimson and J. P. Kane (Tyndale, 1985) has 73 maps, 34 photos, and 34 graphics. Its evangelical perspective, concise and helpful text, and excellent research make it a very good choice, but its greatest strength is its outstanding graphics, such as cross-sections of the Dead Sea.

The Bible Mapbook by Simon Jenkins (Lion, 1984) is much shorter and less expensive than most other atlases, so it offers a good first taste of the usefulness of maps. It contains 91 simple maps, very little text, and 20 graphics. Some of the graphics are computer-generated and intriguing.

The Moody Atlas of Bible Lands by Barry J. Beitzel (Moody, 1984) is scholarly, very evangelical, and full of theological text, indexes, and references. This admirable reference work will be too deep and costly for some, but Beitzel shows vividly how God prepared the land of Israel perfectly for the acts of salvation He was going to accomplish in it.

A ***handbook*** of biblical customs can also be useful. Some good ones are *Today's Handbook of Bible Times and Customs* by William L. Coleman (Bethany, 1984) and the less detailed *Daily Life in Bible Times* (Nelson, 1982).

For Small Group Leaders

The Small Group Leader's Handbook by Steve Barker et al. (InterVarsity, 1982).

Written by an InterVarsity small group with college students primarily in mind. It includes information on small group dynamics and how to lead in light of them, and many ideas for worship, building community, and outreach. It has a good chapter on doing inductive Bible study

Getting Together: A Guide for Good Groups by Em Griffin (InterVarsity, 1982).
Applies to all kinds of groups, not just Bible studies. From his own experience, Griffin draws deep insights into why people join groups; how people relate to each other; and principles of leadership, decision making, and discussions. It is fun to read, but its 229 pages will take more time than the above book.

You Can Start a Bible Study Group by Gladys Hunt (Harold Shaw, 1984).
Builds on Hunt's thirty years of experience leading groups. This book is wonderfully focused on God's enabling. It is both clear and applicable for Bible study groups of all kinds.

How to Build a Small Groups Ministry by Neal F. McBride (NavPress, 1994).
This hands-on workbook for pastors and lay leaders includes everything you need to know to develop a plan that fits your unique church. Through basic principles, case studies, and worksheets, McBride leads you through twelve logical steps for organizing and administering a small groups ministry.

How to Lead Small Groups by Neal F. McBride (NavPress, 1990).
Covers leadership skills for all kinds of small groups—Bible study, fellowship, task, and support groups. Filled with step-by-step guidance and practical exercises to help you grasp the critical aspects of small group leadership and dynamics.

DJ Plus, a special section in *Discipleship Journal* (NavPress, bimonthly).
Unique. Three pages of this feature are packed with practical ideas for small groups. Writers discuss what they are currently doing as small group members and leaders. To subscribe, write to Subscription Services, Post Office Box 54470, Boulder, Colorado 80323-4470.

Bible Study Methods

Braga, James. *How to Study the Bible* (Multnomah, 1982).
Clear chapters on a variety of approaches to Bible study: synthetic, geographical, cultural, historical, doctrinal, practical, and so on. Designed to help the ordinary person without seminary training to use these approaches.

Fee, Gordon, and Douglas Stuart. *How to Read the Bible For All Its Worth* (Zondervan, 1982).
After explaining in general what interpretation (exegesis) and application (hermneneutics) are, Fee and Stuart offer chapters on interpreting

and applying the different kinds of writing in the Bible: Epistles, Gospels, Old Testament Law, Old Testament narrative, the Prophets, Psalms, Wisdom, and Revelation. Fee and Stuart also suggest good commentaries on each biblical book. They write as evangelical scholars who personally recognize Scripture as God's Word for their daily lives.

Jensen, Irving L. *Independent Bible Study* (Moody, 1963), and *Enjoy Your Bible* (Moody, 1962).

The former is a comprehensive introduction to the inductive Bible study method, especially the use of synthetic charts. The latter is a simpler introduction to the subject.

Wald, Oletta. *The Joy of Discovery in Bible Study* (Augsburg, 1975).

Wald focuses on issues such as how to observe all that is in a text, how to ask questions of a text, how to use grammar and passage structure to see the writer's point, and so on. Very helpful on these subjects.

Titles in the LifeChange series:

Genesis
Exodus
Joshua
Ruth & Esther
1 Samuel
Proverbs
Isaiah
Matthew
Mark
Luke
John
Acts
Romans
1 Corinthians
2 Corinthians

Galatians
Ephesians
Philippians
Colossians/Philemon
1 Thessalonians
2 Thessalonians
1 Timothy
2 Timothy
Titus
Hebrews
James
1 Peter
2 Peter and Jude
1, 2, & 3 John
Revelation